THE ULTIMATE
TeaTime Collection

THE ULTIMATE TeaTime Collection

SCONES, SAVORIES, AND SWEETS

hm | books

EDITOR *Lorna Reeves*
GROUP CREATIVE DIRECTOR *Deanna Rippy Gardner*
ART DIRECTOR *Kelly Redding*
SENIOR COPY EDITOR *Rhonda Lee Lother*
EDITORIAL ASSISTANT *Katherine Cloninger*
CREATIVE DIRECTOR/PHOTOGRAPHY *Mac Jamieson*
SENIOR PHOTOGRAPHERS *John O'Hagan, Marcy Black Simpson*
PHOTOGRAPHERS *Jim Bathie, William Dickey, Stephanie Welbourne Steele*
SENIOR DIGITAL IMAGING SPECIALIST *Delisa McDaniel*
DIGITAL IMAGING SPECIALIST *Clark Densmore*

CHAIRMAN OF THE BOARD/CEO *Phyllis Hoffman DePiano*
PRESIDENT/COO *Eric W. Hoffman*
PRESIDENT/CCO *Brian Hart Hoffman*
EXECUTIVE VICE PRESIDENT/CFO *Mary P. Cummings*
EXECUTIVE VICE PRESIDENT/OPERATIONS & MANUFACTURING *Greg Baugh*
VICE PRESIDENT/DIGITAL MEDIA *Jon Adamson*
VICE PRESIDENT/CULINARY & CUSTOM CONTENT *Brooke Michael Bell*
VICE PRESIDENT/SHELTER CONTENT *Cindy Smith Cooper*
VICE PRESIDENT/ADMINISTRATION *Lynn Lee Terry*

Copyright © 2018 by Hoffman Media, LLC
Publishers of *TeaTime* magazine
teatimemagazine.com

All rights reserved. No part of this book may be reproduced or transmitted in any form or by any means, electronic or mechanical, including photocopying, or by any information storage and retrieval system, without permission in writing from Hoffman Media, LLC. Reviewers may quote brief passages.

Hoffman Media, LLC
1900 International Park Drive
Suite 50
Birmingham, AL 35243
hoffmanmedia.com

ISBN 978-1-940772-52-3
Printed in China

ON THE COVER: Raisin-Orange Scones (page 25); Roasted Red Pepper, Goat Cheese, and Walnut Croustades (page 94); Herbed Egg Salad Flower Sandwiches (page 118), Curried Chicken Salad Sandwiches (page 118), Vanilla–Sour Cream Fairy Cakes (page 165); Lemon-Lime Spritz Cookies (page 200); and Blueberry Crumb Bars (page 201)
Recipe Development/Food Styling by Janet Lambert
Styling by Lucy W. Herndon

Contents

Introduction   8
Tea-Steeping Guide   10
Tea-Pairing Guide   12

SCONES   14
Plain Scones   16
Sweet Scones   20
Savory Scones   46
Gluten-Free Scones   54
Delectable Spreads   62

SAVORIES   70
Soups and Salads   72
Quiches and Tartlets   92
Tea Sandwiches and Canapés   114

SWEETS   160
Cakes and Cupcakes   162
Tarts and Cheesecakes   182
Cookies and Bars   198
Other Sweets   218

How-Tos   228
Acknowledgments   236
Recipe Index   238

Introduction

For lovers of afternoon tea, few things could be more enjoyable than a pot of their favorite hot tea accompanied by a three-tiered stand laden with sumptuous scones, succulent tea sandwiches or other savory morsels, and sensational sweet treats. A thoughtful array of shapes, textures, colors, and flavors will make this tower of diminutive foods the perfect focal point for a beautifully set table at any tea party. Featuring more than 175 delectable recipes from the editors of *TeaTime* magazine, *The Ultimate TeaTime Collection* provides a plethora of inspiration and information to make your next teatime a memorable and marvelous occasion. Gluten-free recipes are clearly indicated, so those with special dietary considerations can still indulge in a variety of tasty treats.

Whether the scones are served as the initial course or following the savories, they are sure to delight when served warm and accompanied by a complementary spread. The savory course does not have to be limited to tea sandwiches and canapés. Why not include small servings of soup or salad, petite portions of quiche, or individually sized piquant tartlets? A variety of cakes, dessert tarts, cookies, bars, or candies perched on the top tier will serve as a tempting reminder throughout the afternoon tea of what is in store for the final course.

Because no afternoon tea would be complete without hot tea, an expert tea-pairing guide makes it easy to choose the perfect infusions to accompany each delicious course, and a tea-steeping primer provides instructions for preparing each type. In a day and age when everything seems to move at far too fast a pace, teatime provides an ideal setting for tea lovers to slow down and savor some of the best things in life—relationships, food, and, of course, tea.

Tea-Steeping Guide

The quality of the tea served at a tea party is as important as the food and the décor. To be sure your infusion is successful every time, here are some basic guidelines to follow.

WATER

Always use the best water possible. If the water tastes good, so will your tea. Heat the water on the stove top or in an electric kettle to the desired temperature. A microwave oven is not recommended.

TEMPERATURE

Heating the water to the correct temperature is arguably one of the most important factors in making a great pot of tea. Pouring boiling water on green, white, or oolong tea leaves can result in a very unpleasant brew. Always refer to the tea purveyor's packaging for specific instructions, but in general, use 170° to 195° water for these delicate tea types. Reserve boiling (212°) water for black and puerh teas, as well as herbal and fruit tisanes.

TEAPOT

If the teapot you plan to use is delicate, warm it with hot tap water first to avert possible cracking. Discard this water before adding the tea leaves or tea bags.

TEA

Use the highest-quality tea you can afford, whether loose leaf or prepackaged in bags or sachets. Remember that these better teas can often be steeped more than once. When using loose-leaf tea, generally use 1 generous teaspoon of dry leaf per 8 ounces of water, and use an infuser basket. For a stronger infusion, add another teaspoonful or two of dry tea leaf.

TIME

As soon as the water reaches the correct temperature for the type of tea, pour it over the leaves or tea bag in the teapot, and cover the pot with a lid. Set a timer—usually 1 to 2 minutes for whites and oolongs; 2 to 3 minutes for greens; and 3 to 5 minutes for blacks, puerhs, and herbals. (Steeping tea longer than recommended can yield a bitter infusion.) When the timer goes off, remove the infuser basket or the tea bags from the teapot.

ENJOYMENT

For best flavor, serve the tea as soon as possible. Keep the beverage warm atop a lighted warmer or under your favorite tea cozy if necessary.

Tea-Pairing Guide

CHOOSING A TEA that perfectly complements the menu for afternoon tea is a critical part of hosting a successful event. When selecting infusions to accompany each course, keep in mind that the flavor of the tea should enhance—rather than compete with or overpower—the flavors and mouthfeel of the teatime treats, and vice versa. For that reason, we recommend reserving delicate teas, such as the whites, for drinking on their own. Greens, blacks, and many oolongs are excellent choices for serving alongside food. The following guide offers recommendations of teas to pair with the various flavor profiles of many recipes in this book, but it should by no means be considered definitive:

AUTUMN SPICES Assam Belseri Black, Nepal Ilam Black, Nilgiri Frost Black

CHOCOLATE Golden Monkey Black, Keemun Hao Ya A Black, most fruit-flavored black

HERBS Dragonwell Green, Japanese Sencha Green, Mao Feng Green

RED MEAT Ceylon Uva Highlands Black, Winey Keemun Black, Russian Caravan Black

SMOKED MEAT Irish Breakfast Black Blend, Kenya Black, Vietnam Imperial Oolong

BERRIES China Milk Oolong, Darjeeling 1st Flush Black, Jasmine Green

CITRUS Darjeeling Ambootia Black, Fujian Ti Kuan Yin Oolong, Earl Grey Black

NUTS Da Hong Pao Oolong, Nepal Mist Valley Black, most spice-flavored black

VEGETABLES Keemun Spring Mao Feng Black, Luan Guapian Green, Rwanda Rukeri Black

SPICY Ceylon Highlands Black, Genmaicha Green, Superior Grade Puerh

CHEESE Bohea Black, Ceylon Pettiagalla Estate Black, Gunpowder Green

EGGS & POULTRY Baked Ti Kuan Yin Oolong, Darjeeling 2nd Flush Black, Vietnam Black

OTHER FRUITS Darjeeling Autumnal Black, Fancy Formosa Oolong, Golden Yunnan Black

SEAFOOD Ceylon Lover's Leap Black, Gyokuro Green, Tung Ting Oolong

TROPICAL FRUITS Colombian Black, Jade Oolong, Oriental Beauty Oolong

A prudent host will prepare the chosen tea in advance of the event to verify that the pairing is pleasing and to determine the most beneficial water temperature and steep time. This will ensure good tea and a delightful teatime. For a list of purveyors of fine teas such as these, turn to page 237.

Scones

Plain SCONES

SOUR CREAM SCONES
(recipe on page 19)

Vanilla Scones

> "A Proper Tea is much nicer than a Very Nearly Tea, which is one you forget about afterwards."
>
> — A.A. Milne

Sour Cream Scones

Vanilla Scones
Yield: 12

2 cups self-rising flour
⅓ cup sugar
6 tablespoons cold unsalted butter, cut into pieces
⅓ cup whole buttermilk
¼ cup cold heavy whipping cream
1 large egg
1 tablespoon vanilla extract
1 vanilla bean, split and scraped, seeds reserved
1 egg white, lightly beaten
2 tablespoons vanilla-flavored sugar*

- Preheat oven to 400°.
- Line 2 baking sheets with parchment paper.
- In a large bowl, combine flour and sugar, whisking well. Using a pastry blender, cut butter into flour mixture until mixture resembles coarse crumbs.
- In a medium bowl, combine buttermilk, cream, egg, vanilla extract, and reserved vanilla-bean seeds. Add to flour mixture, stirring until mixture is evenly moist. (Dough will be sticky. If dough seems dry, add more cream, 1 tablespoon at a time.)
- Cut dough in half.
- On a lightly floured surface, roll half of dough into a 6½-inch circle. Cut into 6 wedges. Repeat process with remaining dough. Place scones 2 inches apart on prepared baking sheets.
- Brush scones with egg white, and sprinkle with vanilla-flavored sugar.
- Bake until scones are lightly browned, 9 to 11 minutes.
- Serve warm.

*To make vanilla-flavored sugar, place 1 vanilla bean in a resealable plastic bag, along with desired amount of sugar. Seal bag, and let sit until sugar has absorbed vanilla flavor, approximately 24 hours.

Sour Cream Scones
Yield: 9

2 cups all-purpose flour
¼ cup sugar
2 teaspoons baking powder
1 teaspoon fresh lemon zest
½ teaspoon salt
¼ teaspoon baking soda
4 tablespoons cold salted butter, cut into pieces
½ cup sour cream
¼ cup cold heavy whipping cream

- Preheat oven to 400°.
- Line a baking sheet with parchment paper.
- In a large bowl, combine flour, sugar, baking powder, lemon zest, salt, and baking soda, whisking well. Using a pastry blender, cut butter into flour mixture until mixture resembles coarse crumbs.
- In a small bowl, combine sour cream and whipping cream, whisking to blend. Add to flour mixture, stirring until mixture is evenly moist. (If mixture seems dry, add more cream, 1 tablespoon at a time.) Bring mixture together with hands until a dough forms.
- Turn dough out onto a lightly floured surface. Knead gently 4 to 5 times. Using a rolling pin, roll dough to a 1-inch thickness. Using a 2-inch square cutter, cut 9 scones, rerolling scraps as necessary. Place scones 2 inches apart on prepared baking sheet.
- Bake until scones are lightly browned, 10 to 12 minutes.
- Serve warm.

Sweet SCONES

GINGERY PEACH SCONES
(recipe on page 44)

Blueberry Tea Scones

Blueberry Tea Scones
Yield: 12

1 cup plus 5 tablespoons heavy whipping cream, divided
3 tablespoons blueberry-flavored green tea leaves (from approximately 15 tea bags)
2½ cups all-purpose flour
8 tablespoons sugar, divided
2 teaspoons baking powder
¼ teaspoon salt
⅓ cup cold unsalted butter, cut into pieces
1 large egg, at room temperature
½ cup fresh blueberries
3 tablespoons almond slices
2 tablespoons unsalted butter, melted

- In a small saucepan, heat 1 cup cream over medium heat until just simmering. Remove from heat, add tea leaves, and steep for 10 minutes. Strain, discarding tea leaves. Add enough remaining cream to make 1 cup. Refrigerate until cold, approximately 1 hour.
- Preheat oven to 425°.
- Line a baking sheet with parchment paper.
- In a large bowl, combine flour, 6 tablespoons sugar, baking powder, and salt, whisking well. Using a pastry blender, cut butter into flour mixture until mixture resembles coarse crumbs.
- In a small bowl, combine infused cream and egg, whisking well. Add to flour mixture, stirring until mixture is evenly moist. (If mixture seems dry, add more cream, 1 tablespoon at a time.) Working gently, bring mixture together with hands until a dough forms.
- Turn out dough onto a lightly floured surface, and knead gently several times until smooth. Roll dough to a ½-inch thickness. Using a 2-inch flower-shaped cutter, cut 12 scones, rerolling dough once if needed. Place scones 2 inches apart on prepared baking sheet.
- Brush tops of scones with remaining 5 tablespoons cream. Place 3 or 4 blueberries in the center of each scone. Sprinkle scones with remaining 2 tablespoons sugar. Arrange almond slices as petals on scones.
- Bake until bottom edges of scones are golden brown, 12 to 15 minutes.
- Transfer to a wire rack, and let cool completely. Just before serving, brush with melted butter.

Editor's Note: Please plan ahead. This recipe requires refrigeration.

Blueberry Scones

Blueberry Scones
Yield: 12

2 cups all-purpose flour
⅓ cup sugar
2 teaspoons baking powder
½ teaspoon salt
8 tablespoons cold salted butter, cut into pieces
¾ cup cold heavy whipping cream
1 teaspoon vanilla extract
¼ teaspoon lemon extract
½ cup fresh blueberries

- Preheat oven to 350°.
- Line a baking sheet with parchment paper.
- In large bowl, combine flour, sugar, baking powder, and salt, whisking well. Using a pastry blender, cut butter into flour mixture until mixture resembles coarse crumbs.
- In a liquid-measuring cup, combine cream, vanilla extract, and lemon extract, stirring well. Add to flour mixture, stirring until mixture is evenly moist. (If mixture seems dry, add more cream, 1 tablespoon at a time.) Working gently, bring mixture together with hands until a dough forms.
- Turn dough out onto a lightly floured surface. Knead gently 3 to 4 times. Roll dough to a ½-inch thickness. Scatter ¼ cup blueberries over half of dough. Fold other half of dough over blueberries to enclose them. Lightly roll out dough again to a ½-inch thickness. Repeat scattering, folding, and rolling process with remaining ¼ cup blueberries.
- Using a 2-inch round cutter, cut 12 scones from dough, rerolling scraps as needed. Place scones 2 inches apart on prepared baking sheet.
- Bake until scones are lightly browned, 22 to 24 minutes.
- Serve warm.

BASIC SCONES
how-to on page 228

Apricot Cream Scones

Apricot Cream Scones

Yield: 16

- 2 cups all-purpose flour
- ¼ cup sugar
- 2½ teaspoons baking powder
- ¼ teaspoon salt
- 4 tablespoons cold salted butter, cut into pieces
- ⅓ cup chopped dried apricots
- ½ cup plus 4 tablespoons cold heavy whipping cream, divided
- ½ teaspoon vanilla extract

- Preheat oven to 350°.
- Line a rimmed baking sheet with parchment paper.
- In a large bowl, combine flour, sugar, baking powder, and salt, whisking well. Using a pastry blender, cut butter into flour mixture until mixture resembles coarse crumbs. Add dried apricots, stirring to incorporate.
- In a liquid-measuring cup, combine ½ cup plus 3 tablespoons cream and vanilla extract, stirring to blend. Add to flour mixture, stirring until mixture is evenly moist. (If mixture seems dry, add more cream, 1 tablespoon at a time.) Working gently, bring mixture together with hands until a dough forms.
- Turn out dough onto a lightly floured surface, and knead gently 4 to 5 times. Using a rolling pin, roll dough to a ¾-inch thickness. Using a 1¾-inch fluted round cutter, cut 16 scones from dough, rerolling scraps as needed. Place scones 2 inches apart on prepared baking sheet.
- Brush tops of scones with remaining 1 tablespoon cream.
- Bake until edges of scones are golden and a wooden pick inserted in the centers comes out clean, approximately 16 minutes.
- Serve warm.

Raisin-Orange Scones

Raisin-Orange Scones

Yield: 14 scones

- 2 cups all-purpose flour
- ⅓ cup sugar
- 2 teaspoons baking powder
- 2 teaspoons fresh orange zest
- ½ teaspoon salt
- 4 tablespoons cold salted butter, cut into pieces
- ⅓ cup raisins
- 1 cup cold heavy whipping cream, divided
- ½ teaspoon vanilla extract

- Preheat oven to 350°.
- Line a rimmed baking sheet with parchment paper.
- In a large bowl, combine flour, sugar, baking powder, orange zest, and salt, whisking well. Using a pastry blender, cut butter into flour mixture until mixture resembles coarse crumbs. Add raisins, stirring to combine.
- In a liquid-measuring cup, combine ¾ cup plus 2 tablespoons cream and vanilla extract, stirring to blend. Add to flour mixture, stirring until mixture comes together. (If dough seems dry, add more cream, 1 tablespoon at a time, until dough is uniformly moist.) Working gently, bring mixture together with hands until a dough forms.
- Turn out dough onto a lightly floured surface. Knead gently 3 to 5 times. Using a rolling pin, roll out dough to a ½-inch thickness. Using a 2-inch square cutter, cut 14 scones from dough. Place scones 2 inches apart on prepared baking sheet. Brush tops of scones with remaining 2 tablespoons cream.
- Bake until edges of scones are golden brown and a wooden pick inserted in the centers comes out clean, 18 to 20 minutes.

Strawberry-Lavender Scones

> *"... nowhere is the English genius for domesticity more notably evidenced than in this festival of afternoon tea."*
>
> — George Gissing

Pear Scones

Strawberry-Lavender Scones
Yield: 40

1 cup heavy whipping cream, divided
2 teaspoons culinary lavender
2½ cups sifted bread flour
5 tablespoons sugar
1½ tablespoons baking powder
½ teaspoon salt
¼ teaspoon baking soda
6 tablespoons cold unsalted butter, cut into pieces
½ cup chopped fresh strawberries
½ cup finely chopped toasted almond slivers
2½ tablespoons honey

• In a small microwavable bowl, heat ¾ plus 2 tablespoons cup cream on high in a microwave oven for 30-second intervals until cream simmers. Add lavender, and steep for 5 minutes. Strain, discarding solids. Refrigerate until cold, approximately 1 hour.
• Preheat oven to 400°.
• Line 2 baking sheets with parchment paper.
• In a large bowl, combine flour, sugar, baking powder, salt, and baking soda, whisking well. Using a pastry blender, cut butter into flour mixture until mixture resembles coarse crumbs. Add strawberries and almonds, tossing gently to combine.
• In a liquid-measuring cup, combine honey and lavender-infused cream, stirring well. Add to flour mixture, stirring until mixture is evenly moist. (If mixture seems dry, add more cream, 1 tablespoon at a time.) Working gently, bring mixture together with hands until a dough forms.
• Turn out dough onto a lightly floured surface. Roll dough to a ½-inch thickness. Using a 2-inch square cutter, cut 20 scones, rerolling scraps as needed. Cut squares in half diagonally to form triangles. Place triangular scones 2 inches apart on prepared baking sheets.
• Brush tops with remaining 2 tablespoons cream.
• Bake until scones are light golden brown, 9 to 11 minutes.
• Let cool slightly before serving.

Pear Scones
Yield: 20

2¼ cups self-rising flour
⅓ cup plus 2 tablespoons sugar, divided
½ cup unsalted butter, cut into pieces
1 cup chopped dried pears
⅓ cup whole buttermilk
¼ cup heavy whipping cream
1 large egg, lightly beaten
½ teaspoon vanilla extract
1 large egg white, lightly beaten

• Preheat oven to 400°.
• Line 2 baking sheets with parchment paper.
• In a large bowl, combine flour and ⅓ cup sugar. Using a pastry blender, cut butter into flour mixture until mixture resembles coarse crumbs. Add dried pears, stirring well.
• In a separate bowl, combine buttermilk, cream, egg, and vanilla extract, whisking well. Add to flour mixture, stirring until mixture is evenly moist. (Dough will be sticky. If mixture seems dry, add more cream, 1 tablespoon at a time.)
• On a lightly floured surface, roll dough to a ½-inch thickness. Using a 2¼-inch fluted round cutter, cut 20 scones. Place scones 2 inches apart on prepared baking sheets.
• Brush scones lightly with egg white. Sprinkle evenly with remaining 2 tablespoons sugar.
• Bake until lightly browned, 10 to 12 minutes.

Key Lime Scones

Key Lime Scones

Yield: 12

- 2 cups all-purpose flour
- ⅓ cup plus 1 teaspoon sugar, divided
- 3 tablespoons fresh Key lime zest*
- 2½ teaspoons baking powder
- ½ teaspoon salt
- 4 tablespoons cold salted butter, cut into pieces
- 1 (3-ounce) package cream cheese, cut into small cubes
- ½ cup plus 1 tablespoon cold heavy whipping cream, divided
- 1 large egg, lightly beaten
- 1½ tablespoons fresh Key lime juice*
- 1 teaspoon vanilla extract
- 1 recipe Ginger Curd (recipe on page 66)

- Preheat oven to 350°.
- Line a baking sheet with parchment paper.
- In a medium bowl, combine flour, ⅓ cup sugar, lime zest, baking powder, and salt, whisking well. Using a pastry blender, cut butter and cream cheese into flour mixture until mixture resembles coarse crumbs.
- In a liquid-measuring cup, combine ½ cup cream, egg, lime juice, and vanilla extract, stirring well. Add to flour mixture, stirring until mixture is evenly moist. (If mixture seems dry, add more cream, 1 tablespoon at a time.) Working gently, bring mixture together with hands until a dough forms.
- Turn out dough onto a lightly floured surface, and knead gently 4 to 5 times. Roll dough to a ¾-inch thickness. Using a 2-inch fluted round cutter, cut 12 scones, rerolling scraps as needed. Place scones 2 inches apart on prepared baking sheet.
- Using a pastry brush, lightly brush tops of scones with remaining 1 tablespoon cream. Evenly sprinkle with remaining 1 teaspoon sugar.
- Bake until scones are lightly browned, 18 to 20 minutes.
- Serve warm with Ginger Curd, if desired.

*If Key limes are not available, you may substitute regular limes.

Orange Cream Scones

Yield: 12

- 2½ cups all-purpose flour
- ½ cup plus 2 tablespoons sugar, divided
- 2 teaspoons baking powder
- ½ teaspoon salt
- 8 tablespoons cold salted butter, cut into pieces
- 1 tablespoon fresh orange zest
- ⅔ cup plus 1 tablespoon cold heavy whipping cream, divided
- ½ teaspoon orange extract
- 1 recipe Strawberry Curd (recipe on page 66)

Orange Cream Scones

- Preheat oven to 375°.
- Line a baking sheet with parchment paper.
- In a large bowl, combine flour, ½ cup sugar, baking powder, and salt, whisking well. Using a pastry blender, cut butter into flour mixture until mixture resembles coarse crumbs. Add orange zest, stirring well.
- In a liquid-measuring cup, combine ⅔ cup cream and orange extract. Add to flour mixture, stirring until mixture is evenly moist. (If mixture seems dry, add more cream, 1 tablespoon at a time.) Working gently, bring mixture together with hands until a dough forms.
- On a lightly floured surface, roll dough to a ½-inch thickness. Using a 2¼-inch fluted round cutter, cut 12 scones, rerolling scraps as needed. Place scones 2 inches apart on prepared baking sheet.
- Brush scones with remaining 1 tablespoon cream, and sprinkle with remaining 2 tablespoons sugar.
- Bake until scones are lightly browned, 18 to 20 minutes.
- Serve with Strawberry Curd, if desired.

Hazelnut Wedge Scones

Hazelnut Wedge Scones
Yield: 12 to 16

2½ cups all-purpose flour
⅓ cup granulated sugar
2½ teaspoons baking powder
¼ teaspoon salt
8 tablespoons cold salted butter, cut into pieces
¼ cup finely grated bittersweet chocolate
½ cup toasted chopped hazelnuts
¾ cup cold heavy whipping cream
1 large egg
1 large egg white, lightly beaten
Garnish: castor sugar

• Preheat oven to 350°.
• Line 2 baking sheets with parchment paper.
• In a large bowl, combine flour, granulated sugar, baking powder, and salt, whisking well. Using a pastry blender, cut butter into flour mixture until mixture resembles coarse crumbs. Add chocolate and hazelnuts, stirring to combine.
• In a liquid-measuring cup, combine cream and egg, whisking well. Add to flour mixture, stirring until mixture is evenly moist. (If mixture seems dry, add more cream, 1 tablespoon at a time.) Working gently, bring mixture together with hands until a dough forms.
• Cut dough in half.
• On a lightly floured surface, roll half of dough into a 7-inch circle. Cut into 6 or 8 wedges. Repeat process with remaining dough. Place scones 2 inches apart on prepared baking sheets.
• Brush dough with lightly beaten egg white, and sprinkle with castor sugar, if desired.
• Bake until scones are lightly browned, 20 to 22 minutes.

Cherry-Rose Scones
Yield: 24

2½ cups all-purpose flour
½ cup plus 2 tablespoons sugar, divided
2 teaspoons baking powder
½ teaspoon salt
8 tablespoons cold unsalted butter, cut into pieces
1 (3-ounce) package cold cream cheese, cut into pieces
1 (2-ounce) package dehydrated cherries*, finely chopped
⅓ cup cold heavy whipping cream
1 teaspoon rose water†
½ teaspoon vanilla extract
¼ teaspoon cherry extract

• Preheat oven to 375°.
• Line 2 baking sheets with parchment paper.
• In a large bowl, combine flour, ½ cup sugar, baking powder, and salt, whisking well. Using a pastry blender, cut butter and cream cheese into flour mixture until mixture resembles coarse crumbs. Add cherries, stirring to combine.
• In a liquid-measuring cup, combine cream, rose water, vanilla extract, and cherry extract, stirring well. Add to flour mixture, stirring until mixture is evenly moist. (If mixture seems dry, add more cream, 1 tablespoon at a time.) Working gently, bring mixture together with hands until a dough forms.
• On a lightly floured surface, roll dough to a ¾-inch thickness. Using a 2-inch round cutter, cut 24 scones, rerolling scraps as needed. Place scones 2 inches apart on prepared baking sheets.
• Sprinkle scones evenly with remaining 2 tablespoons sugar.
• Bake until scones are light golden brown, 13 to 15 minutes.
• Serve warm.

*We used Organic Just Cherries, which can be purchased at specialty-foods stores or at justtomatoes.com.

†Rose water can be purchased at Middle Eastern markets, specialty-foods stores, or at americanspice.com.

Cherry-Rose Scones

White Chocolate–Peppermint Scones

White Chocolate–Peppermint Scones
Yield: 10

2 cups all-purpose flour
¼ cup sugar
2 teaspoons baking powder
½ teaspoon salt
4 tablespoons cold salted butter, cut into pieces
½ cup chopped white chocolate
½ cup crushed soft peppermint candies
¾ cup cold heavy whipping cream
½ teaspoon vanilla extract
½ teaspoon peppermint extract
1 recipe Peppermint Cream (recipe on page 64)

- Preheat oven to 350°.
- Line a baking sheet with parchment paper.
- In a large bowl, combine flour, sugar, baking powder, and salt, whisking well. Using a pastry blender, cut butter into flour mixture until mixture resembles coarse crumbs. Add white chocolate and crushed peppermint, stirring to combine.
- In a liquid-measuring cup, combine cream, vanilla extract, and peppermint extract. Add to flour mixture, stirring until mixture is evenly moist. (If mixture seems dry, add more cream, 1 tablespoon at a time.) Working gently, bring mixture together with hands until a dough forms.
- Turn out dough onto a lightly floured surface, and knead gently 4 to 5 times. Roll dough to a ¾-inch thickness. Using a 2-inch round cutter, cut 10 scones, rerolling scraps as needed. Place scones 2 inches apart on prepared baking sheet.
- Bake until scones are light golden brown, 18 to 20 minutes.
- Serve with Peppermint Cream, if desired.

Fig and Honey Scones
Yield: 19

2½ cups sifted bread flour
3 tablespoons sugar
1½ tablespoons baking powder
½ teaspoon salt
6 tablespoons cold unsalted butter, cut into pieces
½ cup chopped dried figs
½ cup finely chopped toasted walnuts
1 cup plus 3 tablespoons cold heavy whipping cream, divided
2½ tablespoons honey

- Preheat oven to 400°.
- Line a baking sheet with parchment paper.
- In a large bowl, combine flour, sugar, baking powder, and salt, whisking well. Using a pastry blender, cut butter into flour mixture until mixture resembles coarse crumbs. Add figs and walnuts, tossing gently to combine.

Fig and Honey Scones

- In a liquid-measuring cup, combine 1 cup plus 2 tablespoons cream and honey, stirring to blend. Add to flour mixture, stirring until mixture is evenly moist. (If mixture seems dry, add more cream, 1 tablespoon at a time.) Working gently, bring mixture together with hands until a dough forms.
- Turn out dough onto a lightly floured surface, and knead gently 4 to 5 times. Roll dough to a ½-inch thickness. Using a 2-inch square cutter, cut 19 scones, rerolling scraps as needed. Place scones 2 inches apart on prepared baking sheet.
- Brush tops of scones with remaining 1 tablespoon cream.
- Bake until scones are light golden brown, 10 to 12 minutes.
- Serve warm.

Chocolate Chip Scones

Chocolate Chip Scones
Yield: 12

2 cups all-purpose flour
⅓ cup plus 1 teaspoon sugar, divided
2 teaspoons baking powder
½ teaspoon salt
6 tablespoons cold salted butter, cut into pieces
1 cup milk chocolate morsels
¾ cup plus 1 tablespoon cold heavy whipping cream, divided
1 large egg yolk
1 teaspoon vanilla extract
1 recipe Strawberry Sweet Cream (recipe on page 64)

• Preheat oven to 350°.
• Line a baking sheet with parchment paper.
• In a large bowl, combine flour, ⅓ cup sugar, baking powder, and salt, whisking well. Using a pastry blender, cut butter into flour mixture until mixture resembles coarse crumbs. Add chocolate morsels, stirring to combine.
• In a liquid-measuring cup, combine ¾ cup cream, egg yolk, and vanilla extract, stirring well. Add to flour mixture, stirring until mixture is evenly moist. (If mixture seems dry, add more cream, 1 tablespoon at a time.) Working gently, bring mixture together with hands until a dough forms.
• On a lightly floured surface, roll dough to a 1-inch thickness. Using a 2¼-inch round cutter, cut 12 scones, rerolling scraps as needed. Place scones 2 inches apart on prepared baking sheet.
• Brush tops of scones evenly with remaining 1 tablespoon cream, and sprinkle with remaining 1 teaspoon sugar.
• Bake until scones are lightly browned, 18 to 20 minutes.
• Serve warm with Strawberry Sweet Cream, if desired.

Chocolate Chip–Cherry Scones
Yield: 12

2½ cups all-purpose flour
½ cup sugar
2 teaspoons baking powder
½ teaspoon salt
8 tablespoons cold unsalted butter, cut into pieces
1 (3-ounce) package cold cream cheese, cut into pieces
¾ cup chopped dried cherries
½ cup mini chocolate morsels
⅓ cup cold heavy whipping cream
1 teaspoon almond extract
½ cup sliced almonds

Chocolate Chip–Cherry Scones

• Preheat oven to 375°.
• Line a baking sheet with parchment paper.
• In a large bowl, combine flour, sugar, baking powder, and salt, whisking well. Using a pastry blender, cut butter and cream cheese into flour mixture until mixture resembles coarse crumbs. Add cherries and chocolate morsels, stirring to combine.
• In a liquid-measuring cup, combine cream and almond extract, stirring well. Add to flour mixture, stirring until mixture is evenly moist. (If mixture seems dry, add more cream, 1 tablespoon at a time.) Working gently, bring mixture together with hands until a dough forms.
• On a lightly floured surface, roll dough to a ¾-inch thickness. Using a 2½-inch heart-shaped cutter, cut 12 scones, rerolling scraps as needed. Place scones 2 inches apart on prepared baking sheet.
• Sprinkle scones with sliced almonds.
• Bake until scones are light golden brown, 13 to 15 minutes.
• Serve warm.

Caramel Scones

Caramel Scones
Yield: 16

2 cups all-purpose flour
⅓ cup firmly packed light brown sugar
1½ teaspoons baking powder
½ teaspoon baking soda
6 tablespoons cold unsalted butter, cut into pieces
¼ cup butterscotch morsels
¼ cup toffee chips
½ cup whole buttermilk
1 large egg
1 teaspoon vanilla extract
Garnish: melted semisweet chocolate

- Preheat oven to 400°.
- Line a baking sheet with parchment paper.
- In a large bowl, combine flour, brown sugar, baking powder, and baking soda, whisking well. Using a pastry blender, cut butter into flour mixture until mixture resembles coarse crumbs. Add butterscotch morsels and toffee chips, stirring to combine.
- In a liquid-measuring cup, combine buttermilk, egg, and vanilla extract, whisking well. Add to flour mixture, stirring until mixture is evenly moist. (If mixture seems dry, add more buttermilk, 1 tablespoon at a time.) Working gently, bring mixture together with hands until a dough forms.
- On a lightly floured surface, roll dough to a ½-inch thickness. Using a 1½-inch square cutter, cut 16 scones, rerolling scraps as needed. Place scones 2 inches apart on prepared baking sheet.
- Bake until scones are light golden brown, 8 to 10 minutes. Let cool on wire racks.
- Place melted chocolate in a small pastry bag fitted with a small round tip. Pipe melted chocolate in a bow design onto scones, if desired.

Sweet Potato Scones
Yield: 8 to 10

1¾ cups all-purpose flour
2 tablespoons firmly packed light brown sugar
2½ teaspoons baking powder
1 teaspoon salt
½ teaspoon baking soda
6 tablespoons cold unsalted butter, cut into pieces
¾ cup sweet potato purée*
⅓ cup whole buttermilk
2 tablespoons honey
1 teaspoon vanilla extract
1 recipe Molasses-Honey Butter (recipe on page 69)

- Preheat oven to 425°.
- Line a baking sheet with parchment paper.
- In a large bowl, combine flour, brown sugar, baking powder, salt, and baking soda, whisking well. Using a pastry blender, cut butter into flour mixture until mixture resembles coarse crumbs.
- In a small bowl, combine sweet potato puree, buttermilk, honey, and vanilla extract, stirring well. Add to flour mixture, stirring until mixture is evenly moist. (If mixture seems dry, add more buttermilk, 1 tablespoon at a time.) Working gently, bring mixture together with hands until a dough forms.
- Turn out dough onto a lightly floured surface, and knead gently 5 times. Roll dough to a ¾-inch thickness. Using a 2-inch square cutter, cut as many scones as possible, rerolling scraps no more than twice. Place scones 2 inches apart on prepared baking sheet.
- Bake until scones are lightly browned, 10 minutes.
- Serve warm with Molasses-Honey Butter, if desired.

*Preheat oven to 425°. Place 1 medium sweet potato on a foil-lined baking sheet. Bake until fork tender, 45 minutes to 1 hour. Remove from oven, and let cool completely, approximately 1 hour. Peel potato, and discard peel. Place potato pulp in the work bowl of a food processor. Process until smooth.

Sweet Potato Scones

Double Chocolate Scones

Double Chocolate Scones
Yield: 12

2 cups all-purpose flour
½ cup unsweetened dark chocolate cocoa powder
  or unsweetened Dutch-process cocoa powder
¼ cup granulated sugar
2 teaspoons baking powder
½ teaspoon fresh orange zest
¼ teaspoon salt
⅓ cup cold unsalted butter, cut into pieces
½ cup dark chocolate chunks
1 cup cold heavy whipping cream
1 large egg
2 tablespoons turbinado sugar

- Preheat oven to 425°.
- Line a baking sheet with parchment paper.
- In a large bowl, combine flour, cocoa powder, granulated sugar, baking powder, orange zest, and salt, whisking well. Using a pastry blender, cut butter into flour mixture until mixture resembles coarse crumbs. Add chocolate chunks, stirring to combine.
- In a liquid-measuring cup, combine cream and egg, whisking well. Add to flour mixture, stirring until mixture is evenly moist. (Dough will be sticky. If mixture seems dry, add more cream, 1 tablespoon at a time.)
- Drop dough by heaping tablespoons 2 inches apart onto prepared baking sheet.
- Sprinkle scones with turbinado sugar.
- Bake until a wooden pick inserted in the centers comes out clean, 8 to 12 minutes. Let cool on baking sheet for 5 minutes.
- Serve warm or at room temperature.

Pistachio Cream Scones
Yield: 12

2 cups all-purpose flour
¼ cup granulated sugar
2 teaspoons baking powder
¼ teaspoon salt
⅓ cup cold unsalted butter, cut into pieces
1 cup finely chopped shelled pistachios
½ cup plus 2 tablespoons cold heavy whipping cream, divided
1 large egg
1 teaspoon lemon zest
1 tablespoon turbinado sugar

- Preheat oven to 425°.
- Line 2 baking sheets with parchment paper.
- In a large bowl, combine flour, sugar, baking powder, and salt, whisking well. Using a pastry blender, cut butter into flour mixture until mixture resembles coarse crumbs. Add pistachios, stirring to combine.
- In a liquid-measuring cup, combine ½ cup cream, egg, and lemon zest, whisking well. Add to flour mixture, stirring until mixture is evenly moist. (If mixture seems dry, add more cream, 1 tablespoon at a time.) Working gently, bring mixture together with hands until a dough forms.
- Turn out dough onto a lightly floured surface, and knead gently 4 to 5 times. Roll dough to a ½-inch thickness. Using a 2-inch star cutter, cut 12 scones, rerolling scraps once if needed. Place scones 2 inches apart on prepared baking sheets.
- Brush tops of scones with remaining 2 tablespoons cream. Sprinkle with turbinado sugar.
- Bake until scones are golden brown, 8 to 10 minutes.
- Serve warm.

Pistachio Cream Scones

Cranberry-Pistachio Scones

Cranberry-Pistachio Scones
Yield: 24

2½ cups sifted all-purpose flour
½ cup plus 2 tablespoons sugar, divided
2 teaspoons baking powder
½ teaspoon salt
8 tablespoons cold salted butter, cut into pieces
1 cup finely chopped dried cranberries
½ cup finely chopped salted pistachios
1 cup plus 3 tablespoons heavy whipping cream, divided

• Preheat oven to 375°.
• Line 2 baking sheets with parchment paper.
• In a large bowl, combine flour, ½ cup sugar, baking powder, and salt. Using a pastry blender, cut butter into flour mixture until mixture resembles coarse crumbs. Add cranberries and pistachios, stirring well. Add 1 cup plus 2 tablespoons cream, stirring until mixture is evenly moist. (If mixture seems dry, add more cream, 1 tablespoon at a time.) Working gently, bring mixture together with hands until a dough forms.
• On a lightly floured surface, roll dough to a ½-inch thickness. Using a 2¼-inch round cutter, cut 24 scones from dough, rerolling scraps if needed. Place scones 2 inches apart on prepared baking sheets.
• Brush tops of scones with remaining 1 tablespoon cream, and sprinkle with remaining 2 tablespoons sugar.
• Bake until lightly browned, 14 to 16 minutes.

Expert Tip
Freeze scones raw on baking sheets. Transfer frozen scones to resealable plastic freezer bags. Bake frozen scones on parchment-lined baking sheets, allowing an additional 5 to 10 minutes for adequate browning to occur.

Pistachio Scones with Sweet Rose Icing
Yield: 12

2 cups all-purpose flour
¼ cup sugar
2 teaspoons baking powder
½ teaspoon salt
4 tablespoons cold salted butter, cut into pieces
⅓ cup finely chopped shelled pistachios
½ cup cold heavy whipping cream
1 teaspoon vanilla extract
1 recipe Sweet Rose Icing (recipe follows)

• Preheat oven to 350°.
• Line a baking sheet with parchment paper.
• In a large bowl, combine flour, sugar, baking powder, and salt, whisking well. Using a pastry blender, cut butter into flour mixture until mixture resembles coarse crumbs. Add pistachios, stirring to combine.
• In a liquid-measuring cup, combine cream and vanilla extract, stirring well. Add to flour mixture, stirring until mixture is evenly moist. (If mixture seems dry, add more cream, 1 tablespoon at a time.) Working gently, bring mixture together with hands until a dough forms.
• Turn out dough onto a lightly floured surface, and knead gently 3 or 4 times. Roll dough to a ¾-inch thickness. Using a 2-inch heart-shaped cutter, cut 12 scones, rerolling scraps as needed. Place scones 2 inches apart on prepared baking sheet.
• Bake until scones are light golden brown, 18 to 20 minutes. Let cool for 2 minutes on baking sheet. Transfer to a wire rack, and let cool slightly.
• Spread Sweet Rose Icing over scones.

Sweet Rose Icing
Yield: approximately ½ cup

½ cup confectioners' sugar
1 tablespoon seedless strawberry preserves
1½ teaspoons water
¼ teaspoon rose water

• In a small bowl, combine confectioners' sugar, preserves, water, and rose water. Whisk until smooth.

Pistachio Scones with
Sweet Rose Icing

Apple and Date Scones

Apple and Date Scones
Yield: 10

- 1½ cups all-purpose flour
- ½ cup quick-cooking oats
- ¼ cup firmly packed light brown sugar
- 2 teaspoons baking powder
- ½ teaspoon salt
- ½ teaspoon ground cinnamon
- 4 tablespoons cold salted butter, cut into pieces
- ¾ cup peeled, finely chopped tart apple
- ½ cup chopped dates
- ¼ cup plus 3 tablespoons cold heavy whipping cream, divided
- 1 large egg, lightly beaten
- ½ teaspoon vanilla extract
- 1 tablespoon turbinado sugar
- 1 recipe Brandied Caramel Cream (recipe on page 64)

- Preheat oven to 350°.
- Line a baking sheet with parchment paper.
- In a large bowl, combine flour, oats, brown sugar, baking powder, salt, and cinnamon, whisking well. Using a pastry blender, cut butter into flour mixture until mixture resembles coarse crumbs. Add apple and dates, stirring well.
- In a liquid-measuring cup, combine ¼ cup and 2 tablespoons cream, egg, and vanilla extract, stirring to blend. Add to flour mixture, stirring until mixture is evenly moist. (If mixture seems dry, add more cream, 1 tablespoon at a time.) Working gently, bring mixture together with hands until a dough forms.
- Turn out dough onto a lightly floured surface, and knead gently 4 to 5 times. Roll dough to a 1-inch thickness. Using a 2-inch round cutter, cut 10 scones, rerolling scraps as needed. Place scones 2 inches apart on prepared baking sheet.
- Lightly brush each scone with remaining 1 tablespoon cream, and sprinkle with turbinado sugar.
- Bake until scones are golden brown, 18 to 20 minutes.
- Serve warm with Brandied Caramel Cream, if desired.

Gingerbread Scones
Yield: 12

- 2 cups self-rising flour
- ¼ cup firmly packed dark brown sugar
- 1½ teaspoons ground ginger
- 1 teaspoon ground cinnamon
- ⅛ teaspoon ground cloves
- 8 tablespoons cold unsalted butter, cut into pieces
- ⅓ cup whole buttermilk
- ⅓ cup unsulfured molasses
- 1 large egg, lightly beaten
- 2 pieces candied ginger, cut into 24 (⅛-inch) squares
- 1 recipe Sweetened Whipped Cream (recipe on page 68)

Gingerbread Scones

- Preheat oven to 400°.
- Line a baking sheet with parchment paper.
- In a large bowl, combine flour, brown sugar, ginger, cinnamon, and cloves, whisking well. Using a pastry blender, cut butter into flour mixture until mixture resembles coarse crumbs.
- In a liquid-measuring cup, combine buttermilk and molasses, stirring to blend. Add to flour mixture, stirring until mixture is evenly moist. (Dough will be sticky. If mixture seems dry, add more buttermilk, 1 tablespoon at a time.)
- Turn out dough onto a lightly floured surface. Pat to a ½-inch thickness. Using a small gingerbread-man cutter, cut 12 scones, rerolling scraps as needed. Place scones 2 inches apart on prepared baking sheet.
- Brush tops of scones with beaten egg. Place 2 candied ginger squares on center of body for buttons.
- Bake until scones are golden brown, 7 to 9 minutes. Transfer to a wire rack, and let cool slightly.
- Serve with Sweetened Whipped Cream, if desired.

Gingery Peach Scones

Gingery Peach Scones

Yield: 16 to 18

2½ cups all-purpose flour
¼ cup granulated sugar
¼ cup firmly packed light brown sugar
2 teaspoons baking powder
½ teaspoon salt
8 tablespoons cold unsalted butter, cut into pieces
1 (3-ounce) package cold cream cheese, cut into pieces
1 (16-ounce) package dried peaches, chopped
¼ cup chopped candied ginger
⅓ cup cold heavy whipping cream
⅔ cup peach nectar, divided
1 teaspoon vanilla extract
½ cup sliced almonds

- Preheat oven to 375°.
- Line 2 baking sheets with parchment paper.
- In a large bowl, combine flour, sugar, brown sugar, baking powder, and salt, whisking well. Using a pastry blender, cut butter and cream cheese into flour mixture until mixture resembles coarse crumbs. Add peaches and ginger, stirring to combine.
- In a liquid-measuring cup, combine cream, ⅓ cup peach nectar, and vanilla extract. stirring to blend. Add to flour mixture, stirring until mixture is evenly moist. (If mixture seems dry, add more cream, 1 tablespoon at a time.) Working gently, bring mixture together with hands until a dough forms.
- On a lightly floured surface, roll dough to a ¾-inch thickness. Using a 3-inch round cutter, cut as many scones as possible, rerolling scraps only once. Place scones 2 inches apart on prepared baking sheets.
- Using a pastry brush, lightly coat scones with remaining ⅓ cup peach nectar. Sprinkle scones evenly with sliced almonds.
- Bake until scones are light golden brown, 13 to 15 minutes.

Pumpkin Scones

Pumpkin Scones

Yield: 12

2½ cups all-purpose flour
½ cup sugar
2½ teaspoons baking powder
1½ teaspoons pumpkin pie spice
½ teaspoon salt
6 tablespoons cold salted butter, cut into pieces
1 cup canned pumpkin
1 large egg, lightly beaten
2 tablespoons cold heavy whipping cream
½ teaspoon vanilla extract
1 recipe Maple Butter (recipe on page 69)

- Preheat oven to 350°.
- Line a baking sheet with parchment paper.
- In a large bowl, combine flour, sugar, baking powder, pumpkin pie spice, and salt, whisking well. Using a pastry blender, cut butter into flour mixture until mixture resembles coarse crumbs.
- In a small bowl, combine pumpkin, egg, cream, and vanilla extract, stirring well. Add to flour mixture, stirring until mixture is evenly moist. (If mixture seems dry, add more cream, 1 tablespoon at a time.) Working gently, bring mixture together with hands until a dough forms.
- Turn out dough onto a lightly floured surface, and knead gently 4 to 5 times. Using a rolling pin, roll dough to a ¾-inch thickness. Using a 2¼-inch round cutter, cut 12 scones, rerolling scraps as needed. Place scones 2 inches apart on prepared baking sheet.
- Bake until scones are lightly golden, 18 to 20 minutes.
- Serve warm with Maple Butter, if desired.

Savory SCONES

ROSEMARY–WHITE CHEDDAR SCONES
(recipe on page 51)

Lemon-Basil Scones

Herbed Scones

Lemon-Basil Scones
Yield: 14

2½ cups all-purpose flour
1 tablespoon sugar
2½ teaspoons baking powder
½ teaspoon salt
½ cup cold salted butter, cut into pieces
2 tablespoons minced fresh basil
1 tablespoon fresh lemon zest
⅔ cup plus 3 tablespoons cold heavy whipping cream, divided

- Preheat oven to 350°.
- Line a baking sheet with parchment paper.
- In a large bowl, combine flour, sugar, baking powder, and salt, whisking well. Using a pastry blender, cut butter into flour mixture until mixture resembles coarse crumbs. Add basil and lemon zest, stirring well. Add ⅔ cup plus 2 tablespoons cream to flour mixture, stirring just until mixture is evenly moist. (If dough seems dry, add more cream, 1 tablespoon at a time.) Working gently, bring mixture together with hands until a dough forms.
- Turn out dough onto a lightly floured surface, and roll to a 1-inch thickness. Using a 2-inch fluted round cutter, cut 14 scones, rerolling scraps as needed. Place scones 2 inches apart on prepared baking sheet.
- Brush tops of scones with remaining 1 tablespoon cream.
- Bake until scones are lightly browned, 17 to 20 minutes.

Herbed Scones
Yield: 12

2 cups self-rising flour
2 tablespoons chopped fresh parsley
1 teaspoon herbes de Provence or other dried mixed herbs
½ teaspoon chopped fresh chives
⅛ teaspoon salt
6 tablespoons cold salted butter, cut into pieces
½ cup whole milk

- Preheat oven to 400°.
- Line a baking sheet with parchment paper.
- In the work bowl of a food processor, combine flour, parsley, herbes de Provence, chives, and salt, pulsing to mix. Add butter, pulsing until mixture resembles coarse crumbs. Add milk, processing until mixture forms a pliable dough. (Be careful not to overmix.)
- Turn out dough onto a lightly floured surface, and roll to a ½-inch thickness. Using a 2-inch round cutter, cut 12 scones, rerolling scraps as needed. Place scones 2 inches apart on prepared baking sheet.
- Bake until scones are golden brown, 14 to 16 minutes.

Caraway-Dill Scones

Caraway-Dill Scones

Yield: 16

2 cups all-purpose flour
2 teaspoons baking powder
½ teaspoon salt
¼ teaspoon ground black pepper
¼ cup cold salted butter, cut into pieces
2 tablespoons chopped fresh dill
2½ teaspoons caraway seeds, divided
1 teaspoon dried dill
1 cup cold heavy whipping cream
1 tablespoon olive oil

- Preheat oven to 350°.
- Line a baking sheet with parchment paper.
- In a medium bowl, combine flour, baking powder, salt, and pepper, whisking well. Using a pastry blender, cut butter into flour mixture until mixture resembles coarse crumbs. Add fresh dill, 2 teaspoons caraway seeds, and dried dill, stirring to combine. Gradually add cream to flour mixture, stirring until mixture is evenly moist. (If mixture seems dry, add more cream, 1 tablespoon at a time.) Working gently, bring mixture together with hands until a dough forms.
- Turn out dough onto a lightly floured surface, and roll to a ½-inch thickness. Using a diamond-shaped cutter, cut as many scones as possible, rerolling scraps once. Place scones 2 inches apart on prepared baking sheet.
- Lightly brush tops of scones with olive oil. Sprinkle remaining ½ teaspoon caraway seeds over tops of scones.
- Bake until scones are light golden brown, 18 to 20 minutes.

Rosemary–White Cheddar Scones

Yield: 12

3 cups all-purpose flour
1 tablespoon baking powder
2 teaspoons chopped fresh rosemary
¼ teaspoon salt
½ cup cold salted butter, cut into pieces
½ cup shredded sharp white Cheddar cheese
1 cup cold heavy whipping cream
1 large egg
1 tablespoon olive oil
¼ teaspoon sea salt
Garnish: fresh rosemary sprigs

- Preheat oven to 400°.
- Line 2 baking sheets with parchment paper.
- In a large bowl, combine flour, baking powder, rosemary, and salt. Using a pastry blender, cut butter into flour mixture until mixture resembles coarse crumbs. Add cheese, tossing to combine.
- In a liquid-measuring cup, combine cream and egg, whisking well. Gradually add to flour mixture, stirring until mixture is evenly moist. (If mixture seems dry, add more cream, 1 tablespoon at a time.) Working gently, bring mixture together with hands until a dough forms.
- Turn out dough onto a lightly floured surface, and roll to a ½-inch thickness. Using a 3-inch round cutter, cut 12 scones, rerolling scraps as needed. Place scones 2 inches apart on prepared baking sheet.
- Brush scones with olive oil, and sprinkle with sea salt.
- Bake until scones are lightly lightly browned, 11 to 13 minutes.
- Garnish with rosemary sprigs, if desired.

Rosemary–White Cheddar Scones

Pimiento-Cheese Scones

• Preheat oven to 450°.
• Line 2 baking sheets with parchment paper.
• In a large bowl, combine flour, baking powder, salt, and baking soda, whisking well. Using a pastry blender, cut butter and cream cheese into flour mixture until mixture resembles coarse crumbs. Add ¼ cup cheese and pimientos, tossing to coat. Make a well in center of flour mixture. Add ¾ cup cream to well, stirring gently with a fork until mixture is uniformly moist. (If mixture seems dry, add more cream, 1 tablespoon at a time.) Working gently, bring mixture together with hands until a dough forms.
• Turn out dough onto a lightly floured surface, and knead gently 3 or 4 times. Roll dough to a ½-inch thickness. Using a 2-inch leaf-shaped cutter, cut 24 scones, rerolling scraps no more than twice. Place scones 2 inches apart on prepared baking sheets.
• Lightly brush scones with remaining 1 tablespoon cream, and sprinkle with remaining ¼ cup cheese.
• Bake until scones are light golden brown, 12 to 15 minutes.

Savory Tomato-Basil Scones
Yield: 16

2 cups self-rising flour
¼ teaspoon salt
¼ teaspoon garlic powder
⅓ cup finely ground dehydrated sun-dried tomatoes
    (not packed in oil)
5 tablespoons cold salted butter, cut into pieces
¼ cup grated pecorino Romano cheese
½ cup chopped fresh basil
1 cup plus 3 tablespoons cold heavy whipping cream, divided
16 thin slices grape tomato

• Preheat oven to 425°.
• Line 2 baking sheets with parchment paper.
• In a large bowl, combine flour, salt, and garlic powder, whisking well. Add sun-dried tomatoes, whisking well. Using a pastry blender, cut butter into flour mixture until mixture resembles coarse crumbs. Add cheese and basil, tossing to combine. Add 1 cup cream, stirring until mixture is evenly moist. (If mixture seems dry, add more cream, 1 tablespoon at a time.) Working gently, bring mixture together with hands until a dough forms.
• Turn out dough onto a lightly floured surface, and gently knead a few times. Pat dough into a ½-inch-thick circle. Cut into 16 wedges. Place wedges 2 inches apart on prepared baking sheets.
• Top each wedge with a tomato slice. Brush tops of wedges with remaining 3 tablespoons cream.
• Bake until golden brown, 6 to 8 minutes.

Pimiento Cheese Scones
Yield: 24

1½ cups all-purpose flour
1½ teaspoons baking powder
½ teaspoon salt
¼ teaspoon baking soda
¼ cup cold unsalted butter, cut into pieces
½ (3-ounce) package cold cream cheese, cut into pieces
½ cup grated sharp Cheddar cheese, divided
½ (4-ounce) jar diced pimientos, drained
¾ cup plus 1 tablespoon cold heavy whipping cream, divided

Savory Tomato-Basil Scones

Gluten-Free SCONES

PECAN-BUTTERSCOTCH SCONES
(recipe on page 60)

Apricot-Almond Scones

Apricot-Almond Scones

Yield: 24

- 2¾ cups gluten-free all-purpose flour
- ¾ cup granulated sugar
- 1 tablespoon baking powder
- 1 teaspoon salt
- 8 tablespoons cold salted butter, cut into pieces
- ¾ cup chopped dried apricots
- ½ cup chopped toasted almonds
- 1¼ cups plus 2 tablespoons cold heavy whipping cream, divided
- 1 teaspoon almond extract
- 2 tablespoons turbinado sugar
- 2 tablespoons chopped sliced almonds

- Preheat oven to 350°.
- Line 2 baking sheets with parchment paper.
- In a large bowl, combine flour, granulated sugar, baking powder, and salt, whisking well. Using a pastry blender, cut butter into flour mixture until mixture resembles coarse crumbs. Add apricots and chopped almonds, tossing to coat with flour.
- In a liquid-measuring cup, combine 1¼ cups cream and almond extract. Add to flour mixture, stirring until mixture is evenly moist. (If mixture seems dry, add more cream, 1 tablespoon at a time.) Bring mixture together with hands until a dough forms.
- Turn out dough onto a lightly floured surface. Roll dough to a ½-inch thickness. Using a 2-inch round cutter, cut 24 scones, rerolling dough as necessary. Place scones 2 inches apart on prepared baking sheets.
- Brush tops of scones with remaining 2 tablespoons cream. Sprinkle with turbinado sugar and sliced almonds.
- Bake until edges are light golden brown, 18 to 20 minutes.

Blueberry-Ginger Scones

Blueberry-Ginger Scones

Yield: 15

- 2¼ cups gluten-free all-purpose flour
- ¾ cup plus 1 teaspoon sugar, divided
- 2 teaspoons baking powder
- 1 teaspoon baking soda
- ½ teaspoon salt
- 6 tablespoons cold salted butter, cut into pieces
- 1 tablespoon minced crystallized ginger
- 1 cup whole buttermilk
- 1 cup fresh blueberries, divided
- 1 tablespoon heavy whipping cream
- 1 recipe Creamy Lemon Curd (recipe on page 66)

- Preheat oven to 400°.
- Line a baking sheet with parchment paper.
- In a large bowl, combine flour, ¾ cup sugar, baking powder, baking soda, and salt, whisking well. Using a pastry blender, cut butter into flour mixture until mixture resembles coarse crumbs. Add ginger, stirring well. Add buttermilk, stirring until mixture is evenly moist. (If mixture seems dry, add more buttermilk, 1 tablespoon at a time.) Bring mixture together with hands until a dough forms.
- Turn out dough onto a a lightly floured surface. Knead dough gently 3 times. Roll dough out to a ½-inch thickness. Scatter ½ cup blueberries over half of dough. Fold remaining half of dough over blueberry half. Gently roll to a ½-inch thickness. Repeat scattering, folding, and rolling process with remaining ½ cup blueberries.
- Using a 2½-inch round cutter, cut 15 scones from dough. Place scones 2 inches apart on prepared baking sheet.
- Brush tops of scones with cream, and sprinkle with remaining 1 teaspoon sugar.
- Bake until light golden brown, approximately 15 minutes.
- Serve warm with Creamy Lemon Curd, if desired.

Editor's Note: See how-to on page 230, or go to teatimemagazine.com to view a step-by-step video.

EXPERT TIP

Freeze gluten-free scones raw on baking sheets. Transfer frozen scones to resealable plastic freezer bags. Bake frozen scones on parchment-lined baking sheets, allowing an additional 5 to 10 minutes for adequate browning to occur.

Dark and White Chocolate Scones

Dark and White Chocolate Scones
Yield: 12

2 cups gluten-free all-purpose flour
¼ cup sugar
1 tablespoon baking powder
½ teaspoon salt
6 tablespoons cold salted butter, cut into pieces
½ cup dark chocolate morsels
¼ cup white chocolate morsels
½ cup cold heavy whipping cream
1 large egg
1 teaspoon vanilla extract
Garnish: ½ cup dark chocolate morsels, melted according to package directions

• Preheat oven to 350°.
• Line a baking sheet with parchment paper.
• In a large bowl, combine flour, sugar, baking powder, and salt, whisking well. Using a pastry blender, cut butter into flour mixture until mixture resembles coarse crumbs. Add dark and white chocolate morsels, tossing to combine.
• In a liquid-measuring cup, combine cream, egg, and vanilla extract, whisking until well blended. Add to flour mixture, stirring until mixture is evenly moist. (If mixture seems dry, add more cream, 1 tablespoon at a time.) Bring mixture together with hands until a dough forms.
• Turn out dough onto a lightly floured surface. Knead gently 2 or 3 times to coat dough with flour. Pat into a 1-inch-thick circle. Cut circle into 12 wedges. Place wedges 2 inches apart on prepared baking sheet.
• Bake until edges of scones are light golden brown, 18 to 20 minutes. Let cool on a wire rack.
• Garnish each wedge with a drizzle of melted dark chocolate, if desired.

Macadamia-Lemon Scones

Macadamia-Lemon Scones
Yield: 20

1½ cups gluten-free all-purpose flour
½ cup sugar
1 tablespoon fresh lemon zest
1¼ teaspoons baking powder
¼ teaspoon baking soda
⅛ teaspoon salt
4 tablespoons cold salted butter, cut into pieces
⅓ cup chopped salted, roasted macadamia nuts
½ cup plus 1 tablespoon whole buttermilk
½ teaspoon lemon extract
2 tablespoons whole milk

• Preheat oven to 350°.
• Line 2 baking sheets with parchment paper.
• In a medium bowl, combine flour, sugar, lemon zest, baking powder, baking soda, and salt, whisking well. Using a pastry blender, cut butter into flour mixture until mixture resembles coarse crumbs. Add macadamia nuts, stirring to combine.
• In a liquid-measuring cup, combine buttermilk and lemon extract. Add to flour mixture, stirring until mixture is evenly moist. (If mixture seems dry, add more buttermilk, 1 tablespoon at a time.) Bring mixture together with hands until a dough forms.
• Turn out dough onto a lightly floured surface. Knead 3 to 4 times. Using a rolling pin, roll dough to a ½-inch thickness. Using a 1¾-inch round cutter, cut 20 scones, rerolling scraps as necessary. Place scones 2 inches apart on prepared baking sheets.
• Brush tops of scones lightly with milk.
• Bake until edges are golden brown and a wooden pick inserted in the centers of scones comes out clean, 13 to 15 minutes.

Zucchini-Parmesan Scones

Pecan-Butterscotch Scones
Yield: 14 to 16

1½ cups gluten-free all-purpose flour
2 teaspoons baking powder
¼ cup granualted sugar
¼ teaspoon salt
¼ cup cold salted butter, cut into pieces
½ cup butterscotch morsels
¼ cup chopped toasted pecans
1 cup cold heavy whipping cream
1 teaspoon vanilla extract
Garnish: turbinado sugar

- Preheat oven to 350°.
- Line a baking sheet with parchment paper.
- In a large bowl, combine flour, baking powder, granulated sugar, and salt, whisking well. Using a pastry blender, cut butter into flour mixture until mixture resembles coarse crumbs. Add butterscotch morsels and pecans, stirring to combine.
- In a liquid-measuring cup, combine cream and vanilla extract. Add to flour mixture, stirring until mixture is evenly moist. (If mixture seems dry, add more cream, 1 tablespoon at a time.) Bring mixture together with hands until a dough forms.
- Using a levered 3-tablespoon scoop, drop dough 2 inches apart onto prepared baking sheet.
- Garnish tops of scones with turbinado sugar, if desired.
- Bake until light golden brown, approximately 20 minutes.

Zucchini-Parmesan Scones
Yield: 16

2½ cups gluten-free all-purpose flour
2½ teaspoons baking powder
½ teaspoon salt
8 tablespoons cold salted butter, cut into pieces
1 cup grated zucchini, squeezed dry
1 cup grated Parmesan cheese
1 cup plus 1 tablespoon cold heavy whipping cream, divided
Garnish: freshly ground black pepper

- Preheat oven to 350°.
- Line 2 baking sheets with parchment paper.
- In a medium bowl, combine flour, baking powder, and salt. Using a pastry blender, cut butter into flour mixture until mixture resembles coarse crumbs. Add zucchini and Parmesan cheese, tossing to combine. Add 1 cup cream, stirring until mixture is evenly moist. (If mixture seems dry, add more cream, 1 tablespoon at a time.) Bring mixture together with hands until a dough forms.
- On a lightly floured surface, roll dough to a ¾-inch thickness. Using a 2¼-inch round cutter, cut 16 scones, rerolling dough as necessary. Place scones 2 inches apart on prepared baking sheet.
- Brush tops of scones with remaining 1 tablespoon cream, and sprinkle with pepper, if desired.
- Bake until lightly browned, 18 to 20 minutes.

GLUTEN-FREE Flour

Many types of gluten-free flours are available today, and we have found that some brands are better for making scones than others. In our test kitchen, we have obtained the best results with Bob's Red Mill Gluten Free 1-to-1 Baking Flour, Cup4Cup Gluten Free Multipurpose Flour, Glutino Gluten Free Pantry All-Purpose Flour, Namaste Perfect Flour Blend, and Pamela's All-Purpose Flour Artisan Blend. Using other brands may yield different results. Always sift or whisk flour before measuring it.

Pecan-Butterscotch Scones

Delectable
SPREADS

MOLASSES-HONEY BUTTER
(recipe on page 69)

Strawberry Sweet Cream

Faux Clotted Cream

Strawberry Sweet Cream
Yield: 1½ cups

1 cup heavy whipping cream
¼ cup confectioners' sugar
½ cup strawberry preserves

- In a medium bowl, combine cream and confectioners' sugar. Beat at medium speed with a mixer until medium peaks form. Add strawberry preserves, gently folding in until well combined.
- Store in an airtight container in the refrigerator until needed.

Faux Clotted Cream
Yield: 1 cup

½ cup heavy whipping cream
1 tablespoon confectioners' sugar
1 tablespoon sour cream

- In a mixing bowl, combine cream and confectioners' sugar. Beat at high speed with a mixer until soft peaks form. Add sour cream, beating at low speed until incorporated and desire consistency is achieved.
- Serve immediately, or store in a covered container in the refrigerator for up to a day.

Brandied Caramel Cream
Yield: 1¼ cups

½ cup heavy whipping cream
¼ cup plus 1 tablespoon caramel topping, divided
2 tablespoons brandy
2 tablespoons confectioners' sugar

- In a medium bowl, combine cream, ¼ cup caramel topping, brandy, and confectioners' sugar. Beat at medium speed with a mixer until soft peaks form.
- Store in a covered container in the refrigerator until needed.
- To serve, swirl remaining 1 tablespoon caramel topping into cream.

Peppermint Cream
(Pictured with White Chocolate–Peppermint Scones on page 33)
Yield: approximately 1½ cups

¾ cup heavy whipping cream
¼ cup crushed soft peppermint candies

- In a mixing bowl, combine cream and crushed peppermint. Beat at medium-high speed with a mixer until medium peaks form.
- Store in an airtight container in the refrigerator until needed.

Brandied Caramel Cream

DELECTABLE SPREADS | *The Ultimate TeaTime Collection* 65

Creamy Lemon Curd

Ginger Curd
Yield: approximately 1½ cups

¾ cup ginger preserves
½ cup firmly packed light brown sugar
¼ cup fresh lemon juice
3 tablespoons unsalted butter, cubed
2 egg yolks
2 large eggs
Garnish: candied ginger

- In the top of a double boiler, combine preserves, brown sugar, lemon juice, and butter. Place over simmering water. Cook just until butter is melted.
- Stirring constantly, add egg yolks and eggs. Cook until thickened, 20 to 30 minutes, stirring occasionally.
- Remove from heat, and strain into a plastic container. Cover top of curd with plastic wrap to prevent it from forming a skin while cooling. Let cool to room temperature.
- Refrigerate for 4 to 6 hours before using. Store in an airtight container in the refrigerator for up to 2 weeks.
- Garnish with candied ginger, if desired.

Strawberry Curd
(Pictured with Orange Cream Scones on page 29)
Yield: 1⅔ cups

1 (16-ounce) package frozen sliced strawberries in syrup, thawed
½ cup sugar
1 tablespoon cornstarch
1 tablespoon fresh lemon juice
3 large egg yolks, lightly beaten
¼ cup salted butter, cut into pieces

- In the work bowl of a food processor or the container of a blender, purée strawberries until smooth. Strain through a fine-mesh sieve. Reserve 1 cup strawberry purée, and discard remainder.
- In a heavy saucepan, combine sugar and cornstarch. Add strawberry purée, lemon juice, and egg yolks. Cook over medium heat until thickened, 5 to 7 minutes, whisking constantly.
- Remove from heat, and gradually add butter, whisking until melted.
- Strain into a plastic container. Cover top of curd with plastic wrap to prevent curd from forming a skin while cooling. Let cool to room temperature.
- Refrigerate for 4 to 6 hours before using. Store in an airtight container in the refrigerator for up to 2 weeks.

Creamy Lemon Curd
Yield: 1 cup

4 large egg yolks
¾ cup sugar
2 tablespoons fresh lemon zest
⅓ cup fresh lemon juice (from approximately 2 large lemons)
¼ cup salted butter, cut into 4 pieces

- In a double boiler or a medium heat-proof bowl set over a pan of simmering water, combine eggs yolks and sugar, whisking until smooth. (Make sure bottom of bowl is not touching water.) Add lemon zest and lemon juice, whisking well. Cook until thickened, 8 to 10 minutes, whisking constantly. (Mixture should coat the back of a spoon.)
- Remove from heat and add butter, one piece at a time, whisking until melted and incorporated. Transfer lemon curd to a small bowl. Place a sheet of plastic wrap on the surface of curd to prevent it from forming a skin while cooling.
- Refrigerate until cold, 4 to 6 hours before using. Store in an airtight container in the refrigerator for up to 2 weeks.

Ginger Curd

DELECTABLE SPREADS | *The Ultimate TeaTime Collection* 67

Apricot-Honey Butter

Apricot-Honey Butter
Yield: approximately 1 cup

¼ cup unsalted butter, softened
¼ cup apricot preserves
¼ cup honey

• In a mixing bowl, beat butter at medium speed with a mixer until smooth and creamy. Add preserves and honey, beating until combined.
• Cover, and refrigerate until ready to serve.

Smoked Paprika Butter
Yield: ½ cup

½ cup salted butter, softened
½ teaspoon smoked paprika

• In a small bowl, combine butter and paprika, stirring well.
• Serve immediately, or transfer butter mixture to a pastry bag fitted with a medium-star tip, and pipe butter rosettes onto a parchment-lined baking sheet. Cover baking sheet with plastic wrap, and refrigerate until firm.
• Transfer butter pats to an airtight container, and refrigerate until needed.

Cracked Pepper and Lemon Double Cream
Yield: approximately ¾ cup

1 (6-ounce) jar double cream*
1 teaspoon fresh finely grated lemon zest
1 teaspoon coarsely ground black pepper
½ teaspoon fine sea salt

• In a small bowl, combine cream, lemon zest, pepper, and salt, stirring until well combined.
• Cover, and refrigerate until ready to serve.

*Double cream, also called Devon cream or clotted cream, is a thick, creamy spread. It is available in the dairy section of some supermarkets and at many specialty-foods stores.

Sweetened Whipped Cream
Yield: 1½ cups

1 cup cold heavy whipping cream
3 tablespoons confectioners' sugar

• In a large bowl, combine cream and confectioners' sugar. Beat at medium-high speed with a mixer until soft peaks form.
• Store in an airtight container in the refrigerator until needed.

Smoked Paprika Butter

Maple Butter
Yield: ½ cup

½ cup salted butter, softened
¼ cup maple syrup

• In a medium bowl, combine butter and maple syrup. Beat at medium speed with a mixer until creamy.
• Store in a covered container in the refrigerator for up to 5 days.

Molasses-Honey Butter
Yield: 1¼ cups

1 cup salted butter, softened
3 tablespoons honey
2 tablespoons molasses

• In a small bowl, combine butter, honey, and molasses. Beat at medium speed with a mixer until smooth, approximately 2 minutes.
• Transfer mixture to a pastry bag fitted with a large star tip. Pipe mixture into desired butter pats.
• Refrigerate until needed.

Savories

Soups AND Salads

GINGER-CARROT SOUP
(recipe on page 84)

Red Quinoa Salad in Frico Cups

Red Quinoa Salad in Frico Cups

Gluten-free | Yield: 12 servings

2 cups cooked red quinoa
½ cup chopped dates
⅓ cup chopped roasted pistachios
¼ cup finely chopped carrot
2 tablespoons chopped green onion (green parts only)
2 tablespoons chopped cilantro
1 recipe Honey-Sherry Vinaigrette (recipe follows)
1 cup watercress
12 Parmesan Frico Cups (recipe on page 79)
Garnish: carrot curl*

• In a medium bowl, combine quinoa, dates, pistachios, carrot, green onion, and cilantro, stirring to blend. Add enough Honey-Sherry Vinaigrette to moisten salad so that it will hold together when scooped. Stir gently to coat.
• Lay watercress leaves in bottoms of frico cups, and top each with a scoop of quinoa salad.
• Garnish each serving with a carrot curl, if desired.
• Serve immediately with remaining vinaigrette on the side, if desired.

*To make carrot curls, draw a vegetable peeler across the side of a peeled carrot.

Honey-Sherry Vinaigrette

Gluten-free | Yield: ½ cup

¼ cup extra-virgin olive oil
¼ cup sherry vinegar*
1 teaspoon fresh lemon juice
1 teaspoon Dijon-style mustard
1 teaspoon finely chopped shallot
1 tablespoon honey
½ teaspoon salt
¼ teaspoon ground black pepper

• In a small jar with a screw-top lid, combine olive oil, vinegar, lemon juice, mustard, shallot, honey, salt, and pepper. Shake vigorously until emulsified. Let stand at room temperature for 30 minutes to allow flavors to develop.
• Use immediately, or refrigerate until needed. (Let come to room temperature before using, shaking again to blend.)

*Use aged sherry vinegar, not sherry cooking wine, which has a higher salt content and a different flavor.

Chilled Cantaloupe Soup

Chilled Cantaloupe Soup

Gluten-free | Yield: 8 (½-cup) servings

4 cups cubed cantaloupe
½ cup fresh orange juice
1 tablespoon fresh lime juice
Garnish: fresh basil leaves, prosciutto*

• In the container of a blender, combine cantaloupe, orange juice, and lime juice. Pulse until well blended and smooth.
• Transfer soup mixture to a covered container, and refrigerate until cold, approximately 4 hours.
• Serve cold.
• Garnish individual servings with fresh basil and prosciutto, if desired.

*If desired, cut small flower shapes from prosciutto for garnish.

Baby English Pea Salad in Artichoke Cups
Gluten-free | *Yield: 6 servings*

1 cup baby (petite) frozen green peas
1 tablespoon finely minced shallot
1 tablespoon sweet pickle relish
2 teaspoons diced pimiento
2 tablespoons finely diced celery
2 teaspoons mayonnaise
1 teaspoon fresh lemon juice
⅛ teaspoon salt
⅛ teaspoon ground black pepper
6 canned artichoke bottoms
Garnish: frisée

- Place frozen green peas in a colander, and hold under hot running tap water for 30 seconds. Shake colander well, and set aside to drain.
- In a medium bowl, combine shallot, pickle relish, pimiento, and celery.
- In a small bowl, combine mayonnaise, lemon juice, salt, and pepper, whisking well.
- Add peas and mayonnaise mixture to shallot mixture, stirring just until combined.
- Cover, and refrigerate until cold, approximately 4 hours.
- Divide salad evenly among artichoke bottoms.
- Garnish with frisée, if desired.

Mushroom-Thyme Soup
Yield: 6 (½-cup) servings

4 tablespoons salted butter
2 cups coarsely chopped white button mushrooms
1 cup chopped sweet onion
2 teaspoons minced garlic
4 tablespoons all-purpose flour
1 (32-ounce) carton beef stock
1 tablespoon fresh thyme leaves
⅛ teaspoon ground nutmeg
⅛ teaspoon ground black pepper
⅓ cup heavy whipping cream
1 tablespoon dry sherry
Garnish: fresh thyme

- In a large saucepan, melt butter over medium-high heat. Add mushrooms and onion, stirring to coat with butter. Reduce heat to low. Cook, stirring occasionally, until vegetables are tender, approximately 8 minutes.
- Add garlic, and cook for 1 minute. Add flour, stirring to blend, and cook for 1 to 2 minutes. Add stock, thyme, nutmeg, and pepper, and bring to a boil. Reduce heat to a simmer. Cook for 30 minutes.
- Add cream and sherry, stirring to incorporate.
- Serve warm.
- Garnish individual servings with fresh thyme, if desired.

"*I live on good soup, not on fine words.*"

—Molière

Mushroom-Thyme Soup

Spring Salad in Frico Cups

Kitchen Tip: *Use preshredded Parmesan cheese to make Parmesan Frico Cups. It bakes into a firmer, sturdier basket.*

Spring Salad in Frico Cups
Gluten-free | Yield: 8 servings

2 cups spring-mix lettuces
¼ cup radish slices
¼ cup matchstick carrots
2 tablespoons thinly sliced green onion
¼ cup fresh green peas
8 Parmesan Frico Cups (recipe below)
1 recipe Herbed Champagne Vinaigrette (recipe follows)

• Divide lettuces, radish slices, carrots, green onion, and green peas evenly among Parmesan Frico Cups. Drizzle salad with Herbed Champagne Vinaigrette.
• Serve immediately with remaining vinaigrette on the side, if desired.

Parmesan Frico Cups
Gluten-free | Yield: varies

¼ cup shredded Parmesan cheese (per frico cup)

• Preheat oven to 350°.
• Line a baking sheet with a silicone baking mat or parchment paper.
• Sprinkle cheese into a 3½- to 4-inch circle on prepared baking sheet. (Make only 8 circles at a time as cheese hardens quickly and becomes difficult to work with.)
• Bake until cheese melts and edges are golden brown, 5 to 8 minutes.
• Using a metal spatula, quickly remove cheese rounds from baking sheet, and drape over an inverted custard cup or the wells of an inverted muffin pan, shaping into ruffled baskets. Let cool completely.
• Remove frico cups from backs of custard cups or muffin pan. Store at room temperature in an airtight container until ready to serve. (Best made day of use.)

Herbed Champagne Vinaigrette
Gluten-free | Yield: ½ cup

¼ cup champagne vinegar
2 teaspoons minced fresh chives
2 teaspoons minced fresh dill
½ teaspoon finely minced shallot
½ teaspoon sugar
¼ teaspoon fine sea salt
⅛ teaspoon ground black pepper
⅓ cup extra-light olive oil

• In a small bowl, combine vinegar, chives, dill, shallot, sugar, salt, and pepper, whisking well. Add olive oil in a slow steady stream, whisking vigorously until emulsified.
• Cover, and let sit at room temperature until ready to use.

Watermelon Gazpacho

Watermelon Gazpacho
Gluten-free | Yield: 8 (1-cup) servings

8 cups puréed watermelon (approximately 2 quarts cubed or ½ large watermelon)
1 cup coarsely chopped red bell pepper
1 cup coarsely chopped English cucumber
1 cup coarsely chopped red onion
¼ cup fresh cilantro leaves
¼ cup fresh lime juice
Garnish: additional fresh cilantro leaves

• In the work bowl of a food processor, combine watermelon, bell pepper, cucumber, onion, cilantro, and lime juice. Pulse until finely chopped. Transfer mixture to an airtight container, and refrigerate until cold, approximately 4 hours.
• Serve cold.
• Garnish individual servings with a cilantro leaf, if desired.

Tomato Gazpacho

Mini Chicken Taco Salad

Tomato Gazpacho

Gluten-free | Yield: 8 (1-cup) servings

5 large ripe tomatoes, peeled and seeded
1 cup coarsely chopped sweet onion
1 cup coarsely chopped English cucumber
½ cup coarsely chopped red bell pepper
½ cup coarsely chopped green bell pepper
½ cup loosely packed parsley leaves
½ cup loosely packed basil leaves
¼ cup canned red pimiento strips
3 tablespoons chopped chives
2 cups beef broth
2 tablespoons fresh lime juice
2 tablespoons fresh lemon juice
1 tablespoon olive oil
1 tablespoon salt
½ teaspoon ground black pepper
Garnish: toasted bread croutons*

- In the work bowl of a food processor or the container of a blender, combine tomatoes, onion, cucumber, bell peppers, parsley, basil, pimiento, chives, broth, lime juice, lemon juice, olive oil, salt, and pepper, pulsing until smooth. (Process in batches, if necessary.)
- Transfer mixture to an airtight container, and refrigerate for 6 hours.
- Serve cold.
- Garnish individual servings with a crouton, if desired.

*Using a small, decorative cutter, cut shapes from bread slices. In a nonstick skillet over medium heat, toast bread shapes on both sides. To make gluten-free, use gluten-free bread.

Mini Chicken Taco Salads

Gluten-free | Yield: 24

24 corn tortillas
3 tablespoons vegetable oil
1 (6-ounce) boneless, skinless chicken breast half
1 tablespoon olive oil
1 teaspoon taco seasoning
¼ teaspoon salt
1 cup finely shredded lettuce
½ cup cooked black beans
¼ cup finely diced red bell pepper
¼ cup finely diced purple onion
1 recipe Creamy Honey-Chipotle Dressing (recipe follows)
Garnish: cilantro leaves

- Preheat oven to 350°.
- Spray 2 (12-well) muffin pans with cooking spray.
- Using a 3½-inch cutter, cut 24 circles from corn tortillas, discarding scraps.
- Working in small batches, wrap tortilla circles in damp paper towels, and place in a microwave oven. Microwave for a few seconds on High (100 percent power) to soften tortilla circles. Press lightly into prepared wells of muffin pans to form a ruffled cup shape. Lightly brush surface of each tortilla cup with vegetable oil.
- Bake until edges are light golden brown, 5 to 7 minutes.
- Remove tortilla cups from muffin pans, and let cool on wire racks. Store in airtight containers until ready to use. (Best made day of use.)
- Brush chicken breast with olive oil, and then sprinkle both sides with taco seasoning and salt.
- Roast in oven until meat is white and opaque with no pink and juices run clear (170° on a meat thermometer), 10 to 15 minutes.
- Let cool, then chop into ¼-inch pieces.
- Fill each shell with lettuce, and top with black beans, bell pepper, onion, and chicken. Drizzle with Creamy Honey-Chipotle Dressing.
- Garnish with cilantro leaves, if desired.
- Serve immediately.

Creamy Honey-Chipotle Dressing

Gluten-free | Yield: 1 cup

1 cup mayonnaise
2 tablespoons honey
1 lime, juiced
¾ teaspoon ground chipotle pepper
¼ teaspoon salt

- In a small bowl, combine mayonnaise, honey, lime juice, chipotle pepper, and salt, whisking until well blended.
- Cover, and refrigerate for up to 2 days until ready to serve.

*"Variety's the very spice of life,
That gives it all its flavor."*

—William Cowper

Watermelon-Feta Salads

White Balsamic Vinaigrette
Gluten-free | Yield: 1 cup

¼ cup white balsamic vinegar
2 tablespoons minced red onion
2 tablespoons minced fresh basil
⅛ teaspoon salt
¾ cup extra-light olive oil

• In a small bowl, combine vinegar, onion, basil, and salt, whisking well. Add olive oil in a slow steady stream, whisking until emulsified. Cover, and refrigerate for up to 2 days until needed.

Creamy Cauliflower-Leek Soup
Gluten-free | Yield: 10 (½-cup) servings

4 tablespoons salted butter
2 cups sliced leeks (white parts only)
1 large head cauliflower, chopped
1 (32-ounce) carton low-sodium chicken stock
½ teaspoon salt
½ cup heavy whipping cream
Garnish: 1 recipe Parmesan Wafers (recipe follows)

• In a large saucepan, melt butter over medium-high heat. Add leeks, and reduce heat to low. Cook until soft, approximately 10 minutes, stirring occasionally.
• Add cauliflower, stock, and salt, and bring to a boil. Reduce heat to simmer. Cook until cauliflower is extremely tender. Remove from heat.
• Using a hand-held immersion blender, purée soup mixture until very smooth. Add cream, stirring to combine.
• Return soup to heat, and let simmer until heated through. Serve warm.
• Garnish individual servings with a Parmesan Wafer, if desired.

Parmesan Wafers
Gluten-free | Yield: 10

⅔ cup grated Parmesan cheese

• Preheat oven to 350°.
• Line a rimmed baking sheet with parchment paper.
• Spread 2 tablespoons cheese into a 1½-inch circle on prepared baking sheet. Repeat 9 times.
• Bake until edges of wafers are golden brown, 5 to 7 minutes. Let cool completely on pan.
• Store wafers in an airtight container. Use the same day.

Watermelon-Feta Salads
Gluten-free | Yield: 6

1 (4½-pound) watermelon
1 (8-ounce) block feta cheese
1 teaspoon ground pink peppercorns
1 recipe White Balsamic Vinaigrette (recipe follows)
Garnish: 6 fresh basil leaves, 6 fresh blueberries

• Cut watermelon into 12 (½-inch) slices. Using a 3-inch flower-shaped cutter, cut a flower shape from each watermelon slice.
• Cut feta into 6 (¼-inch) slices. Using a 3-inch flower-shaped cutter, cut a flower shape from each feta slice.
• Press ground peppercorns decoratively into sides of each feta flower.
• Stack a watermelon flower, a feta flower, and another watermelon flower on top of each other. Cover, and refrigerate for up to a day until needed.
• Drizzle each stack with White Balsamic Vinaigrette.
• Garnish each stack with a basil leaf and a blueberry, if desired.
• Serve immediately with remaining vinaigrette on the side, if desired.

Creamy Cauliflower-Leek Soup

Ginger-Carrot Soup

Petite Potato Salad Flowers
Gluten-free | Yield: 12 servings

6 baby variety potatoes, such as baby Yukon golds
1 teaspoon olive oil
⅛ teaspoon salt
⅛ teaspoon ground black pepper
1 large hard-boiled egg, peeled
¼ cup mayonnaise
1 cup sweet gherkin pickles

• Preheat oven to 400°.
• Line a rimmed baking pan with foil.
• In a medium bowl, toss potatoes with olive oil, salt, and pepper. Spread potatoes on prepared pan, and roast until tender when pierced with the tip of a knife, approximately 20 minutes. Let cool completely.
• Push egg through a fine-mesh sieve.
• In a small bowl, combine mayonnaise and egg, reserving some egg for garnish.
• Using a sharp paring knife, cut 60 very thin (approximately ⅛-inch-thick) slices from pickles, discarding ends.
• Cut each potato in half horizontally. Trim ends of each potato half to level base. Using a melon baller, scoop potato halves, discarding center pulp, to create a cavity. Spoon ½ teaspoon mayonnaise mixture into each cavity.
• Arrange 5 pickle slices in each cavity, overlapping slightly to resemble petals of a flower.
• Garnish center of pickle flowers with a sprinkle of reserved egg.

Make-Ahead Tip: Potatoes can be roasted a day in advance and refrigerated in a covered container. Mayonnaise mixture can be made a day in advance, and refrigerated in a covered container. Pickles can be sliced a day in advance and refrigerated in a covered container with some pickle juice (drain before using). Assemble up to an hour in advance, and refrigerate, covered, until serving time.

Ginger-Carrot Soup
Gluten-free | Yield: 8 (½-cup) servings

2 tablespoons salted butter
1 cup chopped sweet onion
4 cups sliced carrots
1 cup low-sodium chicken stock
1½ teaspoons finely grated fresh ginger root
½ teaspoon ground star anise*
½ teaspoon ground turmeric
Garnish: sour cream

• In a large saucepan, melt butter over medium-high heat. Add onion, and reduce heat to low. Cook, stirring constantly, until onion is caramelized and tender, approximately 10 minutes.
• Add carrots, stock, ginger, anise, and turmeric. Bring to a boil, then reduce heat to a simmer. Cook until carrots are very tender, approximately 30 minutes. Remove soup from heat.
• Using a hand-held immersion blender, purée soup mixture until very smooth. Return soup to heat, and simmer gently until heated through.
• Serve warm.
• Garnish individual servings with sour cream, if desired.

*Grind whole star anise by using a mortar and pestle or an electric spice grinder.

Make-Ahead Tip: Refrigerate in a covered container for up to a day. Reheat in a saucepan over very low heat.

"Never be in a hurry; do everything quietly and in a calm spirit."

— St. Francis de Sales

Petite Potato Salad Flowers

Curried Chicken Salad

Curried Chicken Salad
Gluten-free | *Yield: 8 (½-cup) servings*

½ cup mayonnaise
1 tablespoon fresh lime juice
1 teaspoon honey
½ teaspoon curry powder
½ teaspoon salt
¼ teaspoon ground black pepper
3 cups diced poached chicken
½ cup diced red grapes
½ cup diced yellow apple
⅓ cup diced celery
⅓ cup chopped roasted, salted cashews
Garnish: Bibb lettuce

- In a small bowl, combine mayonnaise, lime juice, honey, curry powder, salt, and pepper, whisking well.
- In a large bowl, combine chicken, grapes, apple, and celery, stirring well. Add mayonnaise mixture, stirring to combine.
- Cover, and refrigerate until cold, at least 4 hours. Add cashews, stirring well.
- Garnish individual servings with Bibb lettuce leaves, if desired.
- Serve immediately.

Make-Ahead Tip: Refrigerate in a covered container for up to 2 days. Add cashews just before serving

Salmon-Filled Cucumbers
Gluten-free | *Yield: 10 servings*

1 (12-inch) English cucumber
⅔ cup sour cream
2 teaspoons fresh lemon zest
¼ teaspoon salt
1 (4-ounce) package thinly sliced smoked salmon
2 tablespoons caviar, such as black lumpfish
Garnish: fresh dill sprigs

- Using a vegetable peeler, scrape cucumber vertically, creating alternating stripes. Trim and discard ends from cucumber. Cut cucumber into 1-inch sections, making sure cuts are straight so that cucumber sections will sit level. Turn each section onto a cut side, and place on a work surface or platter. Using a melon baller, scoop out cucumber sections, discarding center pulp, to create a cavity.

Salmon-Filled Cucumbers

- In a small bowl, combine sour cream, lemon zest, and salt, stirring well. Spoon ½ teaspoon sour cream mixture into each cucumber section.
- Cut smoked salmon into 20 elongated pieces. Arrange 2 salmon pieces in each cucumber section, folding and ruffling to fit cavity. Add a small dollop of remaining sour cream mixture to center of salmon. Top with caviar.
- Garnish with dill sprigs, if desired.

Make-Ahead Tip: Cucumber sections can be scraped, cut, and scooped a day in advance and refrigerated in a resealable plastic bag. Sour cream mixture can be made a day in advance and refrigerated in a covered container. Assemble up to an hour in advance, and refrigerate, covered, until serving time. Garnish just before serving.

Kitchen Tip: To keep fresh dill from wilting, soak in ice water for 10 minutes.

Smoky Chicken and Bean Soup

Smoky Chicken and Bean Soup

Gluten-free | Yield: 8 to 10 servings

1 tablespoon olive oil
1 cup chopped onion
½ cup chopped red bell pepper
½ cup chopped orange bell pepper
½ cup chopped green bell pepper
2 teaspoons finely chopped garlic
4 cups low-sodium chicken stock
2 (15.5-ounce) cans navy beans, rinsed and drained
1 cup canned petite diced tomatoes with liquid
1 teaspoon ground cumin
1 teaspoon dried Mexican oregano leaves*
½ teaspoon salt
¼ teaspoon ground chipotle pepper
¼ teaspoon ground black pepper
1½ cups chopped cooked rotisserie chicken
Garnish: chopped fresh cilantro

• In a medium stockpot, heat olive oil over medium-high heat. Add onion and bell peppers, and reduce heat to medium. Cook, stirring occasionally, until vegetables are crisp-tender, approximately 5 minutes. (Reduce heat again if vegetables start to brown too quickly.) Add garlic during last minute of cooking. Stir, and cook for 1 minute.
• Add chicken stock, beans, tomatoes, cumin, oregano, salt, chipotle pepper, and black pepper. Bring to a boil, stirring occasionally. When mixture reaches a boil, reduce heat to simmer. Cover, and cook for 1 hour, stirring occasionally.
• Add chicken, and cook until chicken is heated through, approximately 5 minutes.
• Serve warm.
• Garnish individual servings with cilantro, if desired.

*Mexican oregano is less sweet than regular oregano. Regular oregano may be substituted for Mexican oregano, if desired.

Make-Ahead Tip: Refrigerate in a covered container for up to 2 days. Reheat in a saucepan over medium heat.

Curried Tomato Soup

Gluten-free | Yield: 8 (½-cup) servings

3 tablespoons olive oil
1 cup chopped red bell pepper
½ cup shallot slices
2 (28-ounce) cans peeled whole tomatoes
2 cups no-salt-added vegetable stock
1 teaspoon ground cumin
1 to 2 teaspoons curry powder
1 teaspoon ground coriander
1 teaspoon salt
½ teaspoon ground paprika
¼ teaspoon ground cinnamon
⅛ teaspoon ground cloves
⅛ teaspoon ground nutmeg
¼ teaspoon ground black pepper
Garnish: plain yogurt, toasted coconut

• In a large saucepan, heat olive oil over medium-high heat. Add bell pepper and shallot. Reduce heat to low, and cook, stirring occasionally, until vegetables are tender, approximately 10 minutes.
• Add tomatoes, breaking apart with a spoon. Add stock, cumin, curry powder to taste, coriander, salt, paprika, cinnamon, cloves, nutmeg, and pepper. Bring to a boil, and then reduce heat to a simmer. Cook for 1½ hours, stirring occasionally. Remove soup from heat.
• Using a hand-held immersion blender, purée soup mixture until smooth. Return soup to heat, and bring to a simmer.
• Serve warm.
• Garnish individual servings with yogurt and toasted coconut, if desired.

Curried Tomato Soup

Sweet Pea Soup

> *"Good manners: The noise you don't make when you're eating soup."*
>
> —Bennett Cerf

Sweet Pea Soup

Yield: 8 (1-cup) servings

- 1 cup thinly sliced leeks (white parts only)
- 5 tablespoons salted butter
- 5 tablespoons all-purpose flour
- 6 cups chicken broth
- 6 cups frozen baby sweet peas
- ⅓ cup heavy whipping cream
- ¼ teaspoon salt
- ⅛ teaspoon ground black pepper
- Garnish: sour cream, fresh pea shoots

- Separate leek slices into rings, and rinse well. Pat dry.
- In a medium saucepan, melt butter over medium heat. Add leeks, and cook until soft, approximately 5 minutes.
- Add flour, whisking constantly until lightly browned, 1 to 2 minutes. Add broth, whisking to combine. Bring mixture to a boil, stirring occasionally.
- Add peas, reduce heat, and simmer for 15 minutes. Remove from heat.
- Using a hand-held immersion blender, purée soup mixture until smooth. Add cream, salt, and pepper, stirring to combine.
- Serve warm.
- Garnish individual servings with sour cream and pea shoots, if desired.

Creamy Yellow Split Pea and Sweet Potato Soup

Creamy Yellow Split Pea and Sweet Potato Soup

Gluten-free | *Yield: 6 (1-cup) servings*

- 1 cup dried yellow split peas
- 2 tablespoons olive oil
- ½ cup chopped sweet onion
- ½ cup finely chopped carrot
- ¼ cup finely chopped celery
- 1 teaspoon chopped garlic
- 2 (32-ounce) cartons low-sodium chicken stock
- 2 cups cubed peeled sweet potatoes
- Salt to taste
- Garnish: minced smoked ham, minced fresh chives

- Soak peas in water for 6 to 8 hours. Drain, and discard water.
- In a large saucepan, heat olive oil over medium-high heat. Add onion, carrot, and celery. Reduce heat to low. Cook, stirring occasionally, until vegetables are tender, 8 to 10 minutes.
- Add garlic, and cook for 1 minute. Add stock, sweet potatoes, and soaked peas. Bring to a boil. Reduce heat to a simmer, and cook until potatoes and split peas are very tender, approximately 2 hours. Remove from heat.
- Using a hand-held immersion blender, purée soup mixture until smooth. Add salt to taste, if desired. Return to heat, and bring to a simmer.
- Serve warm.
- Garnish individual servings with minced ham and fresh chives, if desired.

Make-Ahead Tip: *Refrigerate in a covered container for up to 2 days. Reheat in a saucepan over medium heat.*

Quiches AND Tartlets

SMOKED SALMON CROUSTADES
(recipe on page 101)

Roasted Red Pepper, Goat Cheese, and Walnut Croustades

Make-Ahead Tip: Cheese mixture can be made a day in advance and refrigerated in a covered container. Pepper flowers can be cut a day in advance and refrigerated in a covered container.

Kitchen Tip: Assemble croustades just before serving since shells will become soggy over time. If croustades are not available, pipe mixture onto a cracker, and garnish as suggested.

Tapenade and Cream Cheese Tartlets
Yield: 16

1 cup green pimiento-stuffed olives
¼ cup pitted black olives, such as kalamata
1 small clove garlic
2 tablespoons chopped fresh basil
2 tablespoons chopped fresh parsley
1 tablespoon olive oil
1 teaspoon fresh lemon juice
½ teaspoon fresh thyme leaves
1 (17.5-ounce) package frozen puff pastry (2 sheets), slightly thawed
3 ounces cream cheese, softened
1 teaspoon fresh lemon zest
½ teaspoon heavy whipping cream
1 large egg
1 tablespoon water

- Preheat oven to 400°.
- Line a rimmed baking sheet with parchment paper.
- In the work bowl of a food processor, combine green olives, black olives, garlic, basil, parsley, olive oil, lemon juice, and thyme. Pulse until olives are finely chopped.
- On a lightly floured surface, unfold puff pastry. Using a 1½-inch square cutter, cut 48 squares from puff pastry sheets. Using a 1-inch round cutter, cut and remove center circles from 32 squares to create frames, discarding center circles. Stack 2 frames on top of each solid square. Place stacks 2 inches apart on prepared baking sheet.
- In a small mixing bowl, combine cream cheese, lemon zest, and cream. Beat at medium speed with a mixer until well blended. Transfer cream cheese mixture to a piping bag or a resealable plastic bag with a corner snipped off. Pipe cream cheese mixture evenly into cavity of each puff pastry stack.
- In a small bowl, combine egg and water, whisking well. Lightly brush egg mixture over tops of puff pastry frames.
- Bake until puff pastry is golden brown, 8 to 10 minutes. Let cool slightly.
- Using a finger or a small spoon, press cream cheese centers down into wells. Fill each tartlet with a small amount of tapenade.
- Serve warm or at room temperature.

Roasted Red Pepper, Goat Cheese, and Walnut Croustades
Yield: 24

1 (16-ounce) jar roasted sweet red peppers, divided
11 ounces goat cheese, at room temperature
¾ cup toasted walnut halves
1 tablespoon heavy whipping cream
1 (1.4-ounce) package croustades
Garnish: watercress

- Using paper towels, blot dry ½ cup roasted peppers.
- In the work bowl of a food processor, combine peppers, goat cheese, walnuts, and cream, pulsing until well blended. Refrigerate in a covered container until cold, approximately 4 hours.
- Lay remaining peppers on a cutting board, reserving liquid in jar. Using a linzer-type flower-shaped cutter, cut 24 flowers from peppers. Place in a covered container with enough liquid from jar to cover. Refrigerate until needed. (Blot dry before using as garnish.)
- Place cheese mixture in a piping bag fitted with a medium open-star tip (Wilton #32). Pipe a decorative swirl into each croustade.
- Garnish each canapé with a pepper flower and a watercress sprig, if desired.
- Serve immediately.

Tapenade and Cream Cheese Tartlets

Asparagus-Prosciutto Crustless Quiche

Asparagus-Prosciutto Crustless Quiche

Gluten-free | Yield: 18 pieces

1 pound thin to medium asparagus
6 large eggs
¼ cup grated Parmesan cheese
2 tablespoons minced chives
½ teaspoon salt
½ teaspoon freshly ground black pepper
6 slices prosciutto, each cut into 3 long strips
Garnish: 18 (2-inch-long) chives

- Preheat oven to 400°.
- Line a 9-inch square baking pan with parchment paper.
- Trim asparagus spears to 8 inches in length, discarding tough ends.
- In a large sauté pan, bring 2 inches water to a boil. Immerse asparagus in boiling water for 1 minute to blanch. Transfer asparagus to an ice-water bath to stop the cooking process. Drain asparagus and pat dry.
- In a large bowl, combine eggs, cheese, chives, salt, and pepper, whisking well.
- Layer asparagus in prepared baking pan. Pour egg mixture evenly over asparagus.
- Bake until set, 15 to 20 minutes. Let cool in pan for 10 minutes.
- Turn quiche out onto a cutting board. Cut into 18 (3x1½-inch) rectangles. Wrap each rectangle with a prosciutto strip.
- Garnish each piece with a chive length, if desired.
- Serve immediately.

Arugula, Lemon, and Gruyère Quiche

Yield: approximately 8 servings

½ (14.1-ounce) package refrigerated pie dough (1 sheet)
4 cups arugula
3 large eggs
1½ cups heavy whipping cream
1 tablespoon fresh lemon zest
½ teaspoon salt
¼ teaspoon ground black pepper
¼ teaspoon ground nutmeg
2 cups coarsely shredded Gruyère cheese

- Preheat oven to 450°.
- Lightly spray a 9-inch tart pan with a removable bottom with cooking spray. Unroll pie dough, and press into bottom and up sides of prepared tart pan, trimming and discarding excess dough. Refrigerate for 30 minutes.
- Prick bottom of pie dough with a fork to prevent puffing while baking.
- Bake for 5 minutes. Let cool completely.
- Reduce oven temperature to 350°.
- Place arugula in a colander, and rinse with water.
- Heat a large nonstick sauté pan over high heat. Add wet arugula, stirring and tossing just until wilted and tender, approximately 1 minute. Place arugula in a bowl to cool, and squeeze out excess liquid. Chop finely.
- In a medium bowl, combine eggs, cream, lemon zest, salt, pepper, and nutmeg, whisking until blended.
- Sprinkle cheese into baked tart shell. Arrange arugula evenly over cheese. Pour egg mixture over arugula.
- Bake until quiche is slightly puffed and lightly browned, 38 to 40 minutes. Let cool for 15 minutes before removing from tart pan and serving.

Arugula, Lemon, and Gruyère Quiche

Broccoli Quiche Squares

> "It isn't the great big pleasures that count the most; it's making a great deal out of the little ones."
>
> —Jean Webster

Ham and Chive Quiches
Yield: 8 (4-inch) quiches

1 (14.1-ounce) package refrigerated pie dough (2 sheets)
1 cup diced smoked ham (¼-inch cubes)
1 cup coarsely shredded fontina cheese
3 large eggs
1¼ cups heavy whipping cream
½ teaspoon salt
⅛ teaspoon ground black pepper
2 teaspoons chopped fresh chives

- Preheat oven to 450°.
- On a lightly floured surface, unroll pie dough. Using a 4½-inch round cutter, cut 8 circles from dough. Lightly spray 8 (4-inch) tartlet pans with cooking spray. Press dough rounds into tartlet pans, trimming excess as necessary. Using the large end of a chopstick, press dough into indentations in sides of tartlet pans.
- Place tartlet pans on a rimmed baking sheet. Refrigerate for 30 minutes.
- Prick bottom of pie dough with a fork to prevent puffing while baking.
- Bake until light golden brown, 7 to 8 minutes. Let cool completely before filling.
- Reduce oven temperature to 350°.
- In a small nonstick sauté pan, sear ham over medium-high heat until very lightly browned.
- Place 1 tablespoon ham and 2 tablespoons cheese in each prepared tartlet pan. Set aside.
- In a large liquid-measuring cup, combine eggs, cream, salt, and pepper, whisking well. Divide egg mixture evenly among tartlet pans. Sprinkle each quiche with ¼ teaspoon chives.
- Bake until quiches are set and slightly puffed, 15 to 18 minutes. Let cool slightly before removing from tartlet pans.
- Serve warm or at room temperature for up to 3 hours.

Make-Ahead Tip: *Quiches can be baked a day in advance and stored in a covered container in the refrigerator. Reheat on a rimmed baking sheet in a 350° oven for 6 to 8 minutes.*

Broccoli Quiche Squares
Gluten-free | Yield: 24 servings

½ teaspoon olive oil
¼ cup finely chopped orange bell pepper
2 cups coarsely shredded Gruyère cheese
2 cups cooked fresh broccoli florets, finely chopped
5 large eggs
2 cups heavy whipping cream
½ teaspoon salt
¼ teaspoon ground black pepper
24 square crackers*

- Preheat oven to 350°.
- Spray a shallow 13x9-inch baking pan with cooking spray.
- In a small nonstick skillet, heat olive oil over medium-high heat. Add bell pepper, and cook until tender, 1 to 2 minutes. Set aside.
- Sprinkle 1 cup cheese into prepared baking pan. Scatter broccoli and bell pepper over cheese. Sprinkle remaining 1 cup cheese over vegetables.
- In a medium bowl, combine eggs, cream, salt, and black pepper, whisking well. Pour over cheese and vegetables in baking pan.
- Bake until quiche is set and slightly puffed, approximately 30 minutes. Let cool completely.
- Line a baking sheet with parchment paper.
- Using a 1½-inch square cutter, cut 24 squares from quiche. Place each quiche square on a cracker. Place squares on prepared baking sheet.
- Heat in oven until warm, approximately 5 minutes.
- Serve immediately.

*For a gluten-free version of this recipe, use gluten-free crackers, or serve without crackers.

TARTLET CRUST
how-to on page 232

Ham and Chive Quiches

TARTLET CRUST
how-to on page 232

Tomato-Feta Tartlets

Tomato-Feta Tartlets

Yield: 8

1 (14.1-ounce) package refrigerated pie dough (2 sheets)
½ cup mayonnaise
½ cup plus 2 tablespoons crumbled feta cheese, divided
2 tablespoons chopped fresh basil
¼ teaspoon ground black pepper
1 cup red grape tomatoes
1 cup yellow grape tomatoes
Garnish: fresh basil

- Preheat oven to 450°.
- On a lightly floured surface, unroll pie dough. Using a 4½x2½-inch tartlet pan as a guide, cut 8 shapes from dough. Lightly spray 8 tartlet pans with cooking spray. Press dough shapes into prepared tartlet pans, trimming excess as necessary. Using the large end of a chopstick, press dough into indentations in sides of tartlet pans.
- Place tartlet pans on a rimmed baking sheet. Refrigerate for 30 minutes.
- Prick tartlet dough with a fork to prevent puffing during baking.
- Bake for 5 minutes. Let cool completely.
- Reduce oven temperature to 350°.
- In a small bowl, combine mayonnaise, ½ cup cheese, basil, and pepper, stirring to blend. Divide mayonnaise mixture evenly among prepared tartlet shells, spreading evenly.
- Cut tomatoes in half lengthwise. Divide tomato halves evenly among prepared tartlet shells, and arrange vertically in a shingled fashion. Sprinkle remaining 2 tablespoons cheese over tomatoes.
- Bake tartlets until tomatoes have softened and are tender, approximately 10 minutes. When cool enough to handle, remove from tartlet pans. Serve warm or at room temperature.
- Garnish each with fresh basil, if desired.

Make-Ahead Tip: Tartlet shells can be made earlier in the day and stored in an airtight container until needed.

Smoked Salmon Croustades

Smoked Salmon Croustades

Yield: 24

1 (8-ounce) package cream cheese, softened
2 tablespoons finely chopped fresh dill
2 teaspoons fresh lemon zest
2 teaspoons fresh lemon juice
¼ teaspoon salt
¼ teaspoon ground black pepper
24 mini croustades
2 (4-ounce) packages thinly sliced smoked salmon
Garnish: fresh dill

- In a medium mixing bowl, combine cream cheese, dill, lemon zest, lemon juice, salt, and pepper. Beat at high speed with a mixer until well blended.
- Transfer cream cheese mixture to a piping bag fitted with a medium open-star tip (Wilton #21). Pipe enough mixture into each croustade to cover bottom in an even layer.
- Cut smoked salmon into ¾-inch strips of varying lengths, but no longer than 2 inches. Arrange salmon strips in concentric circles in each croustade to form a rose.
- Pipe a cream cheese rosette into center of each salmon rose.
- Garnish each croustade with a fresh dill sprig, if desired.

Make-Ahead Tip: Cheese mixture can be made a day in advance and refrigerated in a covered container until needed. For ease of piping, let soften before using. Croustades can be assembled an hour in advance and stored, covered, in the refrigerator. Garnish just before serving.

TARTLET CRUST
how-to on page 232

Kale and Sausage Quiches

"Each cup of tea represents an imaginary voyage."

—Catherine Douzel

Apricot-Chive Chicken Slad in Puff Pastry Shells

Kale and Sausage Quiches
Yield: 12

1 (14.1-ounce) package refrigerated pie dough (2 sheets)
1 tablespoon olive oil
3 cups coarsely chopped curly kale
¾ cup shredded fontina cheese
¾ cup grated Parmesan cheese
¾ cup crumbled, cooked pork breakfast sausage
3 large eggs
1 cup heavy whipping cream
¼ teaspoon salt
¼ teaspoon ground black pepper
⅛ teaspoon ground nutmeg

• Preheat oven to 450°.
• On a lightly floured surface, unroll pie dough. Using a 4½-inch round cutter, cut 12 circles from dough. Lightly spray 12 (4-inch) tartlet pans with cooking spray. Press dough rounds into tartlet pans, trimming excess as necessary. Using the large end of a chopstick, press dough into indentations in sides of tartlet pans.
• Place tartlet pans on a rimmed baking sheet. Refrigerate for 30 minutes.
• Prick bottom of pie dough with a fork to prevent puffing while baking.
• Bake until light golden brown, 7 to 8 minutes. Let cool completely before filling.
• Reduce oven temperature to 350°.
• In a medium sauté pan, heat olive oil over medium-high heat until oil shimmers. Add kale, and cook until wilted and tender. Let cool.
• In each prepared tartlet pan, layer 1 tablespoon each fontina cheese, Parmesan cheese, sausage, and kale.
• In a large liquid-measuring cup, combine eggs, cream, salt, pepper, and nutmeg, whisking well. Divide egg mixture evenly among tartlet pans.
• Bake until quiches are set and slightly puffed, 15 to 18 minutes. Let cool slightly before removing from tartlet pans.
• Serve warm or at room temperature for up to 3 hours.

Make-Ahead Tip: *Quiches can be baked a day in advance and stored in a covered container in the refrigerator. Reheat on a rimmed baking sheet in a 350° oven for 6 to 8 minutes.*

Apricot-Chive Chicken Salad in Puff Pastry Shells
Yield: 8

2 cups chopped cooked chicken
½ cup chopped dried apricots
2 tablespoons toasted slivered almonds
1 tablespoon chopped fresh chives
¾ cup mayonnaise
1 tablespoon lemon juice
¼ teaspoon salt
⅛ teaspoon ground black pepper
8 frozen puff pastry shells, thawed and baked according to package directions
Garnish: apricot roses*, fresh chives

• In a large bowl, combine chicken, apricots, almonds, chives, mayonnaise, lemon juice, salt, and pepper, stirring well. Cover, and refrigerate until just before serving.
• Divide chicken salad evenly among puff pastry shells.
• Garnish with an apricot rose and a chive, if desired.
• Serve immediately.

*To make apricot roses, slice dried apricots lengthwise into thin slices. Roll slices into rosettes.

Make-Ahead Tip: *Apricot-Chive Chicken Salad can be made a day in advance and refrigerated until needed. Add almonds just before serving.*

TARTLET CRUST how-to on page 232

Lobster Salad Barquettes
Yield: 6

3 (5-ounce) lobster tails
1 cup water
1 tablespoon salt
2 tablespoons mayonnaise, such as Hellman's
2 tablespoons fresh lemon juice
2 tablespoons minced celery
1 tablespoon minced red onion
⅛ teaspoon salt
½ (14.1-ounce) package refrigerated pie dough (1 sheet)
Garnish: lemon peel curls

• Insert a skewer lengthwise along top of each lobster tail to prevent curling during steaming.
• In a medium saucepan with a steamer basket, bring water and salt to a boil. Place prepared lobster tails in steamer basket, and steam, covered, until shells turn pink and meat is opaque white, 7 to 8 minutes. Remove lobster tails from steamer, and let cool slightly until cool enough to handle.
• Using kitchen scissors, cut lobster tails along back of shell, pull open, and remove lobster meat. Chop meat into ½-inch pieces.
• In a small bowl, combine lobster, mayonnaise, lemon juice, celery, onion, and salt, tossing until mixed. Cover, and refrigerate until cold, 3 to 4 hours.
• Preheat oven to 450°.
• On a lightly floured surface, unroll pie dough. Using a 4½x1½-inch barquette tartlet pan as a guide, cut 6 shapes from dough. Lightly spray 6 tartlet pans with cooking spray. Press dough shapes into prepared tartlet pans, trimming excess as necessary. Using the large end of a chopstick, press dough into indentations in sides of tartlet pans.
• Place tartlet pans on a rimmed baking sheet. Refrigerate for 30 minutes.
• Prick tartlet dough with a fork to prevent puffing during baking.
• Bake until golden brown, 7 to 9 minutes. Let cool on wire racks. Carefully remove tartlet shells from pans.
• When ready to serve, divide lobster salad among prepared tartlet shells.
• Garnish each with a lemon peel curl, if desired.

Spinach-Artichoke Phyllo Cups
Yield: 30

1 teaspoon olive oil
1 (6-ounce) bag fresh baby spinach
¼ cup finely chopped canned artichoke hearts
3 tablespoons mayonnaise
2 tablespoons sour cream
⅔ cup freshly finely grated Parmesan cheese
⅛ teaspoon garlic salt
⅛ teaspoon ground black pepper
⅛ teaspoon ground red pepper
30 frozen mini phyllo cups, thawed

• Preheat oven to 350°.
• In a large nonstick sauté pan, heat olive oil over medium-high heat. Add spinach, stirring until wilted and tender, 1 to 2 minutes.
• Transfer spinach to a bowl. Using kitchen scissors, cut spinach into small pieces. Drain any remaining liquid.
• To spinach, add artichokes, mayonnaise, sour cream, Parmesan cheese, garlic salt, black pepper, and red pepper, stirring to combine. Evenly divide spinach mixture among phyllo cups. Place filled phyllo cups on a rimmed baking sheet.
• Bake until filling is hot and cheese melts, 10 to 12 minutes.
• Serve immediately.

Spinach-Artichoke Phyllo Cups

Mushroom and Three-Cheese Tartlets

Mushroom and Three-Cheese Tartlets
Yield: 12

1¾ cups finely chopped toasted pecans
1¾ cups crumbled round buttery crackers
7½ tablespoons butter, divided
1 large egg white
1 (10-ounce) package goat cheese, at room temperature
1 (8-ounce) package cream cheese, softened
1½ cups heavy whipping cream
3 large eggs
2 cups shredded Swiss cheese
1 tablespoon all-purpose flour
¾ teaspoon kosher salt, divided
½ teaspoon ground black pepper, divided
1½ tablespoons olive oil
4 cups assorted wild mushrooms, cleaned and trimmed

• Preheat oven to 325°.
• In a medium bowl, combine pecans, crackers, 6 tablespoons butter, and egg white, stirring well. Press into bottoms of a 12-well mini cheesecake pan.
• Bake for 10 minutes. Let cool completely in pan on a wire rack.
• In a large bowl, combine goat cheese and cream cheese. Beat at medium speed with a mixer until smooth. Add cream, beating to combine. Add eggs, one at time, beating well after each addition. Add Swiss cheese, flour, ½ teaspoon salt, and ¼ teaspoon pepper. Divide batter evenly among prepared wells of pan.
• Bake until set, approximately 20 minutes. Let cool in pan for 30 minutes. Refrigerate for at least 2 hours.
• Remove tartlets from pan, and place on a rimmed baking sheet.
• Preheat oven to 350°.
• Warm tartlets in oven for 5 to 8 minutes.
• Meanwhile, in a nonstick skillet, heat olive oil and remaining 1½ tablespoons butter over medium-high heat. Add mushrooms. Season with remaining ¼ teaspoon salt and remaining ¼ teaspoon pepper. Cook for 5 minutes without stirring. Stir mushrooms to sear all sides. Remove from pan, and drain on paper towels.
• Top warm tartlets with hot mushrooms.
• Serve immediately.

Fresh Herb and Gruyère Quiche
Yield: approximately 8 servings

½ (14.1-ounce) package refrigerated pie dough (1 sheet)
1 cup coarsely shredded Gruyère cheese
2 tablespoons finely chopped fresh dill
2 tablespoons finely chopped fresh chives
1 tablespoon fresh thyme leaves
3 large eggs
1 cup heavy whipping cream
¼ teaspoon salt
¼ teaspoon ground black pepper

• Preheat oven to 450°.
• Lightly spray a 9-inch tart pan with a removable bottom (or a 9-inch pie plate) with cooking spray. Unroll pie dough, and press into bottom and up sides of prepared tart pan, trimming and discarding excess dough. Refrigerate for 30 minutes.
• Prick bottom of pie dough with a fork to prevent puffing while baking.
• Bake until light golden brown, 5 to 7 minutes. Let cool completely before filling.
• Spread cheese in bottom of cooled crust. Sprinkle evenly with dill, chives, and thyme.
• In a medium mixing bowl, combine eggs, cream, salt, and pepper, whisking well. Pour egg mixture over cheese and herbs in tart pan.
• Bake until quiche is set, approximately 25 minutes. Let cool slightly before removing from pan.
• Serve warm.

Kitchen Tip: *Gruyère is more expensive than Swiss cheese but well worth the extra money. It provides a rich nutty flavor that Swiss cheeses do not.*

Kitchen Tip: To remove quiche from bottom of tart pan, use a cake lifter or a wide thin-bladed spatula.

Fresh Herb and Gruyère Quiche

Coq au Vin Tartlets

Coq au Vin Tartlets
Yield: 8

1 (14.1-ounce) package refrigerated pie dough (2 sheets)
½ cup sliced white button mushrooms
1 teaspoon olive oil
¼ teaspoon dried thyme
⅛ teaspoon salt
⅛ teaspoon ground black pepper
½ cup pearl onions
2 tablespoons salted butter
2 tablespoons all-purpose flour
1 cup beef stock
2 tablespoons red wine
1 tablespoon finely chopped cooked bacon
½ cup chopped roasted chicken
Garnish: fresh thyme

- Preheat oven to 450°.
- On a lightly floured surface, unroll pie dough. Using a 4½x2½-inch tartlet pan as a guide, cut 8 shapes from dough. Lightly spray 8 tartlet pans with cooking spray. Press dough shapes into prepared tartlet pans, trimming excess as necessary. Using the large end of a chopstick, press dough into indentations in sides of tartlet pans.
- Place tartlet pans on a rimmed baking sheet. Refrigerate for 30 minutes.
- Prick tartlet dough with a fork to prevent puffing during baking.
- Bake until edges are golden brown, 5 to 7 minutes. Let cool completely before removing from pans.
- Reduce oven temperature to 350°.
- In a small bowl, combine mushrooms, olive oil, thyme, salt, and pepper, tossing to coat. On another rimmed baking sheet, spread mushrooms in a single layer.
- Bake until mushrooms are tender and release their juices, approximately 20 minutes.
- In a medium sauce pan, bring 2 inches water to a boil. Immerse pearl onions in boiling water for 1 minute to blanch. Transfer onions to an ice-water bath to stop the cooking process. Drain onions and pat dry.
- In a small sauté pan, melt butter over medium-high heat. Add flour, whisking constantly. Cook until a smooth paste forms, 1 to 2 minutes, reducing heat if mixture starts to brown. Add beef stock, whisking and cooking over medium-low heat until mixture is smooth and creamy. Add wine and bacon, stirring to incorporate. Add chicken, pearl onions, and roasted mushrooms, stirring to combine and cooking until heated through, 2 to 3 minutes. Spoon chicken mixture into cooled tartlet shells. Serve immediately.
- Garnish each with a sprinkle of fresh thyme leaves and a thyme sprig, if desired.

Make-Ahead Tip: Tartlet shells, roasted mushrooms, and beef gravy may be made a day in advance. Store tartlet shells in an airtight container at room temperature. Refrigerate mushrooms and gravy in separate airtight containers. Reheat gravy over low heat before adding remaining ingredients. If gravy is too thick, add more beef stock to thin.

Apricot, Pecan, and Brie Phyllo Cups

Apricot, Pecan, and Brie Phyllo Cups
Yield: 15

15 pecan halves
1 teaspoon olive oil
⅛ teaspoon salt
⅛ teaspoon ground red pepper
4 ounces Brie cheese, rind removed
15 frozen phyllo cups, thawed
3 teaspoons apricot jam

- Preheat oven to 350°.
- In a small bowl, combine pecans and olive oil, tossing to coat. Place pecans right side up on a rimmed baking sheet. Sprinkle evenly with salt and red pepper.
- Bake until lightly toasted, 4 to 5 minutes. Let cool completely. Chop finely.
- Divide Brie evenly among phyllo cups. Top each evenly with jam. Place filled phyllo cups on a rimmed baking sheet.
- Bake until Brie melts, 5 to 6 minutes.
- Divide chopped pecans among prepared phyllo cups. Serve warm.

Make-Ahead Tip: *Artichoke Frittata can be baked up to 3 hours in advance and served at room temperature.*

Artichoke Frittata

Artichoke Frittata

Gluten-free | Yield: approximately 8 servings

5 large eggs
¾ cup whole milk
1 tablespoon salted butter, melted
1½ teaspoons chopped fresh oregano
½ teaspoon fresh lemon zest
¼ teaspoon ground black pepper
1 (14-ounce) can artichoke hearts, drained, chopped, and squeezed dry
½ cup shredded sharp provolone cheese
Garnish: mascarpone cheese, fresh oregano sprig

- Preheat oven to 375°.
- Spray a shallow 9-inch glass pie plate with cooking spray.
- In a medium bowl, combine eggs, milk, melted butter, chopped oregano, lemon zest, and pepper, whisking to blend. Add artichokes and provolone cheese, stirring until incorporated. Pour into prepared pie plate.
- Bake until frittata is set and slightly puffed, approximately 23 minutes. Let cool slightly before removing from pie plate. Serve warm or at room temperature.
- Garnish with a swirl of mascarpone cheese and an oregano sprig, if desired.

Creamy Crab-Artichoke Tartlets

Yield: 8

½ (14.1-ounce) package refrigerated pie dough (1 sheet)
2 tablespoons salted butter
2 tablespoons all-purpose flour
1 cup heavy whipping cream
½ cup whole milk
1 cup lump crabmeat
⅓ cup finely chopped canned artichoke hearts
2 tablespoons diced pimientos
1 tablespoon finely chopped green onion (green tops)
1 tablespoon finely chopped parsley
1 tablespoon dry sherry
½ teaspoon salt
¼ teaspoon ground black pepper
⅛ teaspoon ground nutmeg
Garnish: finely grated Parmesan cheese, ground paprika

- Preheat oven to 450°.
- On a lightly floured surface, unroll pie dough. Using a 2¾-inch round cutter, cut 8 rounds from pie dough. Lightly spray 8 (2½-inch) tartlet pans with cooking spray. Press dough rounds into prepared tartlet pans, trimming excess. Using the large end of a chopstick, press dough into indentations in sides of tartlet pans.

Creamy Crab-Artichoke Tartlets

TARTLET CRUST how-to on page 232

- Place tartlet pans on a rimmed baking sheet. Refrigerate for 30 minutes.
- Prick tartlet dough with a fork to prevent puffing during baking.
- Bake until golden brown, 5 to 7 minutes. Let cool completely. Carefully remove tartlet shells from pans. Store in an airtight container at room temperature until ready to fill.
- In a medium nonstick sauté pan, melt butter over medium heat. Add flour, whisking and cooking for 3 minutes until a smooth paste forms. Add cream and milk, whisking until smooth. Add crab, artichokes, pimiento, green onion, parsley, sherry, salt, pepper, and nutmeg, stirring to blend. Cook over low heat until heated through, approximately 5 minutes. Divide warm crab mixture among prepared tartlet shells. Serve immediately.
- Garnish each with a sprinkle of Parmesan cheese and paprika, if desired.

Make-Ahead Tip: Crab mixture can be made a day in advance and refrigerated in a covered container. Rewarm gently over low heat. Tartlet shells are best made the same day.

Goat Cheese, Date, and Prosciutto Phyllo Cups

Goat Cheese, Date, and Prosciutto Phyllo Cups
Yield: 15

4 ounces goat cheese, at room temperature
4 ounces cream cheese, softened
¼ cup coarsely chopped prosciutto
¼ cup coarsely chopped dates
1 tablespoon heavy whipping cream
2 teaspoons fresh thyme leaves
¼ teaspoon ground black pepper
15 frozen phyllo cups, thawed
Garnish: fresh thyme sprigs

• In the work bowl of a food processor, combine goat cheese, cream cheese, prosciutto, dates, cream, thyme, and pepper. Pulse until well blended and prosciutto and dates are finely chopped enough to pass through a piping tip.
• Transfer mixture to a piping bag fitted with a large open-star tip (Wilton #1M). To prevent cups from becoming soggy, pipe cheese mixture into phyllo cups just before serving.
• Garnish each with a fresh thyme sprig, if desired.

Make-Ahead Tip: Cheese mixture can be made a day in advance and refrigerated in a covered container until needed. For ease of piping, let soften before using.

Poppyseed Chicken Tartlets
Yield: 20

1 (14.1-ounce) package refrigerated pie dough (2 sheets)
4 tablespoons salted butter
4 tablespoons all-purpose flour
1½ cups chicken stock
¼ teaspoon ground black pepper
¼ cup sour cream
1 tablespoon finely chopped fresh tarragon
1 tablespoon poppy seeds
1 tablespoon lemon juice
2 cups chopped, cooked chicken
Garnish: finely chopped toasted pecans

• Preheat oven to 450°.
• On a lightly floured surface, unroll pie dough. Using a 2¾-inch round cutter, cut 20 rounds from pie dough. Lightly spray 20 (2¼-inch) tartlet pans with cooking spray. Press dough rounds into prepared tartlet pans, trimming excess. Using the large end of a chopstick, press dough into indentations in sides of tartlet pans.
• Place tartlet pans on a rimmed baking sheet. Refrigerate for 30 minutes.
• Prick tartlet dough with a fork to prevent puffing during baking.
• Bake until golden brown, 5 to 7 minutes. Let cool completely. Carefully remove tartlet shells from pans. Store in an airtight container at room temperature until ready to fill.
• In a large nonstick sauté pan, melt butter over medium heat. Add flour, whisking and cooking for 3 minutes until a smooth paste forms. Add stock and pepper, whisking until smooth. Add sour cream, tarragon, poppy seeds, and lemon juice, whisking until incorporated. Add chicken, and cook until heated through. Divide warm chicken mixture among prepared tartlet shells. Serve immediately.
• Garnish with chopped pecans, if desired.

Make-Ahead Tip: Chicken mixture can be made a day in advance and refrigerated in an airtight container. Rewarm gently over low heat. Tartlet shells are best made the same day.

Poppyseed Chicken Tartlets

TARTLET CRUST
how-to on page 232

TEA Sandwiches AND Canapés

TARAGON-SHRIMP SALAD FINGER SANDWICHES
(recipe on page 133)

CUCUMBER CANAPÉS
(recipe on page 124)

Creole Egg Salad Tea Sandwiches

Make-Ahead Tips *for* Tea Sandwiches

• In general, fillings and spreads for tea sandwiches can be made a day in advance. Refrigerate in a covered container until needed.
• Bread shapes for tea sandwiches can be cut a day in advance and stored in a resealable plastic bag at room temperature.
• Tea sandwiches can be assembled a few hours ahead and refrigerated in a covered container until serving time. Be sure to cover sandwiches with damp paper towels so they don't dry out before serving.
• For even layers when making triple-stack sandwiches, measure filling, and spread equal amounts between bread slices.
• To create clean cuts, wipe knife between each cut.
• When using a cutter, it is easier to make neat cuts if bread is frozen. Let thaw before serving.
• Add any garnishes just before serving.

Ham Salad Triple Stacks

Creole Egg Salad Tea Sandwiches
Yield: 12

8 large hard-boiled eggs, peeled
⅓ cup mayonnaise
3 tablespoons Creole mustard
¼ cup finely chopped celery
3 tablespoons dill pickle relish
¼ teaspoon ground black pepper
12 large slices multigrain bread, frozen
Garnish: watercress

• In a medium bowl and using a pastry blender, chop eggs into small pieces. Add mayonnaise, mustard, celery, pickle relish, and pepper, stirring to blend. Cover, and refrigerate until cold, approximately 4 hours.
• Using a 3¾-x-2-inch diamond-shaped cutter, cut 24 shapes from frozen bread slices, discarding scraps.
• Divide egg salad evenly among 12 bread diamonds. Top with remaining bread diamonds. Cover with damp paper towels, and let bread thaw completely (approximately 30 minutes) before serving.
• Garnish each tea sandwich with watercress, if desired.

Ham Salad Triple Stacks
Yield: 16

1 (1.5-pound) center-cut ham steak, prepared according to package instructions and cooled
½ cup mayonnaise
⅓ cup golden raisins
⅓ cup finely chopped celery
2 tablespoons finely chopped fresh chives
1 tablespoon fresh lemon juice
16 slices rye sandwich bread, frozen
8 slices pumpernickel sandwich bread, frozen
Garnish: fresh chives

• In the work bowl of a food processor, process ham until finely chopped.
• In a medium bowl, combine chopped ham, mayonnaise, raisins, celery, chives, and lemon juice, stirring until well blended. Set aside.
• Using a 2-inch hexagonal-shaped cutter, cut 32 shapes from frozen rye bread slices and 16 shapes from frozen pumpernickel bread slices, discarding scraps.
• Spread 1 tablespoon ham salad onto a rye bread shape. Top with a pumpernickel bread shape, and spread another 1 tablespoon ham salad. Top with another rye bread shape to create a triple-stack sandwich. Repeat with remaining bread shapes and ham salad. Cover with damp paper towels, and let bread thaw completely (approximately 30 minutes) before serving.
• Garnish with chives, if desired.

Herbed Egg Salad Flower Sandwiches

> *"Come let us have some tea and continue to talk about happy things."*
>
> —Chaim Potok

- In a medium bowl and using a pastry blender, chop eggs into fine pieces. Add mayonnaise, dill, mustard, chives, parsley, salt, and pepper, stirring to combine.
- Spread egg salad onto whole flower-shaped bread pieces, and top with bread pieces with centers removed. Fill sandwich centers with additional egg salad.
- Garnish each sandwich with a dill sprig, if desired.

Curried Chicken Salad Sandwiches
Yield: 12

6 slices firm wheat bread
3 cups very finely chopped roast chicken
¾ cup mayonnaise
½ cup very finely chopped green apple
¼ cup very finely chopped celery
¼ cup finely chopped toasted slivered almonds
1 tablespoon fresh lime juice
¾ teaspoon curry powder
¼ teaspoon salt
¼ teaspoon ground black pepper

- Using a 2¼-inch square cutter, cut 12 shapes from bread. Using a serrated bread knife, cut each square in half diagonally. To prevent bread from drying out, cover with damp paper towels, or store in a resealable plastic bag.
- In a medium bowl, combine chicken, mayonnaise, apple, celery, almonds, lime juice, curry powder, salt, and pepper, stirring until mixture is thoroughly blended.
- Spread chicken salad onto 12 bread triangles. Top each with another bread triangle.

Kitchen Tip: Process chicken in a food processor to achieve a fine texture. Use meat pulled from a rotisserie chicken to save time.

Herbed Egg Salad Flower Sandwiches
Yield: 12

12 slices firm white sandwich bread, frozen
8 hard-cooked eggs, peeled
⅓ cup mayonnaise
2 tablespoons finely chopped fresh dill
1 tablespoon Dijon-style mustard
1 tablespoon finely chopped fresh chives
1 tablespoon finely chopped fresh parsley
½ teaspoon salt
¼ teaspoon ground black pepper
Garnish: fresh dill sprigs

- Using a 2¼-inch flower-shaped cutter, cut 24 shapes from frozen bread slices. Using a ¾-inch round cutter, cut out centers from 12 of the flower shapes. To prevent bread from drying out, cover with damp paper towels, or store in a resealable plastic bag.

Curried Chicken Salad Sandwiches

TEA SANDWICHES AND CANAPÉS *The Ultimate TeaTime Collection*

Olive-Pecan Finger Sandwiches

Olive-Pecan Finger Sandwiches
Yield: 12

1 (8-ounce) package cream cheese, softened
1 tablespoon heavy whipping cream
3 tablespoons finely chopped pimiento-stuffed green olives
2 tablespoons finely chopped pitted black olives
¼ cup finely chopped toasted pecans
12 slices very thin whole-wheat sandwich bread

• In a medium mixing bowl, combine cream cheese and cream. Beat at medium speed with a mixer until smooth. Add green olives, black olives, and pecans, stirring by hand until incorporated.
• Spread cream cheese mixture onto a bread slice. Top with another bread slice, and spread with cream cheese mixture. Top with a third bread slice to make a triple-stack sandwich. Repeat with remaining bread slices and cream cheese mixture.
• Using a serrated bread knife in a gentle sawing motion, trim and discard crusts from sandwiches. Cut each sandwich into 3 rectangles.
• Serve immediately, or cover with damp paper towels, place in a covered container, and refrigerate for a few hours until serving time.

Make-Ahead Tip: Cream cheese mixture can be made a day in advance and refrigerated in a covered container until needed. Let come to room temperature before using.

Crab Cake Crostini
Yield: 22

1 (8-ounce) container fresh, pasteurized lump crabmeat
1 cup panko (Japanese bread crumbs), divided
1 large egg
1 tablespoon minced red bell pepper
1 tablespoon mayonnaise
1 tablespoon fresh lemon juice
1 teaspoon minced shallot
¼ teaspoon salt
⅛ teaspoon ground black pepper
⅓ cup olive oil
1 recipe Lemon-Lime Aïoli (recipe follows)
22 prepared French bread crostini
Garnish: chives, red bell pepper flowers*

• In a medium bowl, combine crabmeat, ¼ cup panko, egg, minced bell pepper, mayonnaise, lemon juice, shallot, salt, and pepper, stirring to blend. Divide crabmeat mixture into 22 equal portions. Shape each portion into a cake, and coat with remaining ¾ cup panko. Place crab cakes on a rimmed baking sheet, and refrigerate for 30 minutes.
• In a large nonstick skillet, heat olive oil over medium-high heat. When oil is hot, cook crab cakes in batches until golden brown, 1 to 2 minutes per side. Drain on paper towels.
• Spoon ¼ teaspoon Lemon-Lime Aïoli onto each crostini, and top with a crab cake. Top each crab cake with another ¼ teaspoon aïoli.
• Garnish each canapé with chives and a bell pepper flower*, if desired.
• Serve immediately.

*Using a small flower-shaped cutter, cut shapes from fresh bell pepper sections.

Make-Ahead Tip: Crab cakes can be pan-fried and then refrigerated until needed. To warm, place on a parchment-lined baking sheet, and heat for 5 minutes in a 350° oven.

Lemon-Lime Aïoli
Gluten-free | Yield: ¼ cup

¼ cup mayonnaise
½ teaspoon fresh lime zest
½ teaspoon fresh lemon zest
1 teaspoon fresh lime juice
1 teaspoon fresh lemon juice

• In a small bowl, combine mayonnaise, zests, and juices, whisking to blend. Cover, and refrigerate until needed, up to a day.

Crab Cake Crostini

Pickled Egg Canapés

Pickled Egg Canapés
Yield: 24

6 medium eggs
1 (15-ounce) can sliced beets, drained and juice reserved for pickling liquid, beets reserved for Apple-Beet Slaw
6 tablespoons white distilled vinegar
2 tablespoons firmly packed light brown sugar
¼ teaspoon whole allspice berries
¼ teaspoon salt
12 slices firm white sandwich bread, frozen
2 tablespoons salted butter, softened
1 recipe Apple-Beet Slaw (recipe follows)

- In a medium saucepan, place eggs, and cover with water. Bring to a boil over high heat, and reduce heat so that water boils gently. Cook, uncovered, for exactly 7 minutes. Remove from heat, and transfer eggs to a bowl filled with ice and water. When eggs are completely cooled, crack shells, and carefully peel away shells. Set aside.
- In a small saucepan, combine reserved juice from beets, vinegar, brown sugar, allspice berries, and salt, and bring to a boil over medium-high heat. Reduce heat, and simmer for 5 minutes. Remove from heat, and let liquid cool to room temperature.
- Place eggs in a large, wide-mouth canning jar. (Don't crowd or pack eggs.) Pour cooled pickling liquid over eggs, making sure that eggs are completely submerged and surrounded by liquid. Screw on lid. Refrigerate for 3 days.
- Preheat oven to 350°.
- Using a 2½-inch triangular cutter, cut 24 shapes from frozen bread slices, discarding crusts. Cover with damp paper towels, and let bread thaw slightly (approximately 15 minutes). Place on a rimmed baking sheet. Spread bread triangles lightly with butter.
- Bake until edges are light golden brown, approximately 7 minutes. Let cool completely.
- Remove eggs from pickling liquid, and blot dry on paper towels. Using an egg slicer, cut slices from eggs. Set aside.
- Divide Apple-Beet Slaw among toast triangles. Top each canapé with a pickled egg slice.
- Serve immediately.

Make-Ahead Tip: *Plan ahead, and make pickled eggs at least 3 days in advance. Slaw can be made a day in advance. Toast triangles should be made the same day and stored in a resealable plastic bag.*

Kitchen Tip: *When making hard-boiled eggs, don't use very fresh eggs, as they are more difficult to peel. Keep uncooked eggs in the refrigerator for 1 to 2 weeks to "age" before boiling, or using a straight pin or a thumbtack, gently pierce rounded end of each egg before boiling—or to ensure good results, do both.*

Apple-Beet Slaw
Gluten-free | Yield: 1½ cups

Beets reserved from Pickled Egg Canapés recipe (recipe above), finely chopped
½ cup finely chopped red apple
⅓ cup finely chopped celery
1 tablespoon finely chopped fresh parsley
1 tablespoon finely chopped green onion (green parts only)
2 tablespoons red wine vinegar
1 tablespoon olive oil
1 tablespoon Dijon-style mustard
¼ teaspoon sugar
¼ teaspoon salt
⅛ teaspoon ground black pepper

- In a medium bowl, combine beets, apple, celery, parsley, and green onion, stirring to blend. Set aside.
- In a small jar with a screw-top lid, combine vinegar, olive oil, mustard, sugar, salt, and pepper, shaking vigorously until emulsified. Add vinaigrette to beet mixture, tossing to coat. Cover, and refrigerate until cold, approximately 4 hours.

> *"When tea becomes ritual, it takes its place at the heart of our ability to see greatness in small things."*
>
> —Muriel Barbery,
> *The Elegance of the Hedgehog*

Cucumber Canapés

Cucumber Canapés
Yield: 18

9 slices firm white sandwich bread
2 English cucumbers
¼ cup mayonnaise
½ teaspoon fresh lemon zest
½ teaspoon fresh lemon juice
¼ teaspoon salt
Garnish: watercress

• Using a serrated knife in a gentle sawing motion, trim and discard crusts from bread. Cut each bread slice into 2 (2½-x-1½-inch) pieces. Cover with damp paper towels, or store in a resealable plastic bag to keep from drying out while preparing other ingredients.
• Trim ends from cucumbers, and cut into 1½-inch sections. Slice each section vertically to yield 54 cucumber slices in all. Set aside.
• In a small bowl, combine mayonnaise, lemon zest, lemon juice, and salt, whisking until blended. Spread ¼ teaspoon mayonnaise mixture onto each bread slice. Top with 3 cucumber slices, overlapping evenly.
• Garnish each canapé with watercress, if desired.

Make-Ahead Tip: Prepare canapés up to 4 hours before serving, cover with damp paper towels, and refrigerate in an airtight container.

Apple, Ham, and Gouda Tea Sandwiches
Yield: 12

12 slices rye-pumpernickel-swirl bread, frozen
12 thin slices Gouda cheese
½ cup mayonnaise
3 tablespoons whole-grain Dijon-style mustard
1 cup baby kale leaves
12 very thin slices smoked ham
12 very thin slices green apple
Garnish: additional slices green apple

• Using a 2¼-inch square cutter, cut 24 squares from frozen bread slices, discarding scraps. Cover with damp paper towels, or store in a resealable plastic bag to prevent drying out while preparing other ingredients.
• Using the same square cutter as for bread, cut 12 squares from cheese slices.
• In a small bowl, combine mayonnaise and mustard, stirring to blend. Spread aïoli onto each bread square.
• Using 12 bread squares (aïoli side up) as a base, assemble 12 sandwiches, stacking ingredients in the following order: kale, cheese, ham (ruffled and gathered to fit bread), apple slice, and another bread square (aïoli side down). Cover with damp paper towels, and let bread thaw completely (approximately 30 minutes) before serving.
• Garnish each tea sandwich with a few apple slices, if desired.

Kitchen Tip: Cut apple slices just before assembling and serving. If making sandwiches a few hours in advance, brush apple slices with lemon juice to prevent browning.

Apple, Ham, and Gouda Tea Sandwiches

Tomato, Basil, and Bacon Canapés

Beef au Poivre and Watercress Tea Sandwiches
Yield: 6 to 8

1 (6-ounce) beef tenderloin fillet
1 teaspoon whole black peppercorns
1 teaspoon whole green peppercorns
1 teaspoon whole white peppercorns
¼ cup plus 2 teaspoons butter, softened, divided
¼ cup sliced shallot
1 tablespoon plus 1 teaspoon olive oil, divided
¼ teaspoon garlic salt
6 to 8 small Parkerhouse rolls
⅓ cup watercress

- Preheat oven to 350°.
- Line a baking sheet with foil.
- Remove beef from refrigerator, and let stand at room temperature for 30 minutes before cooking.
- Coarsely chop or grind peppercorns, and combine in a small bowl.
- In a sauté pan, heat 2 teaspoons butter over medium-high heat. Add shallot, and reduce heat to low. Cook, stirring occasionally, until shallot is soft and lightly browned. Let cool. Chop finely, and set aside.
- Drizzle beef with 1 tablespoon olive oil. Season with garlic salt. Press peppercorns onto all sides of beef.
- In a small oven-safe sauté pan or a cast-iron skillet, heat remaining 1 teaspoon olive oil over high heat. Add beef, and sear on all sides until browned and lightly charred, approximately 2 minutes per side. Transfer beef to prepared baking sheet.
- Bake for 5 minutes for rare, longer for a greater degree of doneness. (Fillet will feel very springy when pressed with a finger after cooking for a short time; this indicates a rare interior. If meat feels very firm when pressed, it is more well done.) Wrap beef in foil, and let stand for 15 minutes before slicing.
- Using a sharp knife, slice across grain into ¼-inch slices. Set aside.
- In a small bowl, combine cooled shallot and remaining ¼ cup butter, stirring until combined.
- Slice rolls in half horizontally. Spread shallot butter on insides of rolls. Arrange a beef slice over bottom half of each roll (ruffling to fit roll), and tuck in a piece of watercress. Top with remaining halves of rolls (buttered side down).
- Serve immediately.

Make-Ahead Tip: Beef fillet can be cooked in advance and refrigerated for up to a day. Before serving, heat in a 350° oven just until warm, approximately 5 minutes.

Tomato, Basil, and Bacon Canapés
Yield: 24

12 slices firm wheat sandwich bread, frozen
2 tablespoons mayonnaise
24 small leaves fresh basil
24 slices cherry tomato (approximately 8 tomatoes)
2 tablespoons crumbled cooked bacon

- Using a 1½-inch square cutter, cut 24 squares from frozen bread slices, discarding crusts. Cover with damp paper towels, and let bread thaw completely (approximately 30 minutes).
- Spread ¼ teaspoon mayonnaise onto each bread square. Top each with a basil leaf, a tomato slice, and ¼ teaspoon bacon.
- Serve immediately, or cover with slightly damp paper towels to prevent drying out, and refrigerate for up to 30 minutes.

Beef au Poivre and Watercress Tea Sandwiches

Smoked Tuna Tea Sandwiches

> *"There are few hours in life more agreeable than the hour dedicated to the ceremony known as afternoon tea."*
>
> —Henry James, *The Portrait of a Lady*

Mango Chutney–Cucumber Flower Canapés

CUCUMBER FLOWER
how-to on page 231

Smoked Tuna Tea Sandwiches
Yield: 12

1 (12-ounce) can albacore tuna, drained
2 tablespoons mayonnaise
2 tablespoons finely chopped celery
1 tablespoon chopped green onion
1 tablespoon sour cream
1½ teaspoons finely ground Lapsang Souchong dry tea leaves*
1 teaspoon fresh lemon juice
¼ teaspoon Worcestershire sauce
⅛ teaspoon salt
⅛ teaspoon ground black pepper
12 slices light rye bread, frozen
½ cup arugula leaves
12 slices Campari tomato
¾ cup loosely packed alfalfa sprouts
Garnish: arugula leaves, frilled pick

• In a medium bowl, combine tuna, mayonnaise, celery, green onion, sour cream, ground tea, lemon juice, Worcestershire sauce, salt, and pepper, stirring until blended. Transfer mixture to a covered container, and refrigerate until well chilled, approximately 4 hours.
• Using a 2¼-inch round cutter, cut 24 rounds from frozen bread slices, discarding scraps. Cover with damp paper towels, or store in a resealable plastic bag to prevent drying out while preparing other ingredients.
• Using 12 bread rounds as a base, assemble 12 sandwiches, stacking ingredients in the following order: 3 arugula leaves, tuna mixture, 1 tomato slice, sprouts, and another bread round. Cover with damp paper towels, and let bread thaw completely (approximately 30 minutes) before serving.
• Garnish each tea sandwich with an arugula leaf and a frilled pick, if desired.

*Lapsang Souchong is a very smoky-flavored Chinese black tea.

Mango Chutney–Cucumber Flower Canapés
Yield: 12

4 slices firm white sandwich bread, frozen
2 tablespoons mango chutney
1 English cucumber

• Using a 1¾-inch round cutter, cut 12 rounds from frozen bread, discarding crusts. Cover with damp paper towels, and let bread thaw slightly (approximately 15 minutes).
• Spread each bread round very thinly with mango chutney.
• Trim ends from cucumber. Using a mandoline, cut 48 very thin slices from cucumber.
• Fold each cucumber slice into quarters. Place 5 folded slices upright on each bread round, unfolding slightly to resember flower petals.

Kitchen Tip: A mandoline is essential for cutting paper-thin slices of cucumber. For testing purposes, we used a Kyocera mandoline, available at Sur La Table (surlatable.com).

Broccoli Salad Roulades
Yield: 12 to 14 (1-inch) slices

2 cups finely chopped broccoli florets
¼ cup finely chopped red bell pepper
¼ cup coarsely grated carrot
¼ cup finely crumbled cooked bacon
2 tablespoons finely chopped dried cherries
1 tablespoon finely diced purple onion
1 recipe White Balsamic Dressing (recipe follows)
2 large flour tortillas

- In a medium bowl, combine broccoli, bell pepper, carrot, bacon, cherries, onion, and White Balsamic Dressing, stirring well. Set aside.
- Lay tortillas on a work surface. Divide broccoli salad evenly between tortillas, placing salad in a long row in the center of each. Roll tortillas up firmly into cylinders, enclosing salad.
- Using a serrated knife, cut off ends of each rolled-up tortilla to make a neat cylinder approximately 6 to 7 inches long. Wrap each firmly with plastic wrap, and refrigerate for at least 30 minutes and up to 2 hours.
- Remove plastic wrap, and cut roulades into 1-inch slices.
- Serve immediately.

White Balsamic Dressing
Gluten-free | Yield: ½ cup

½ cup mayonnaise
2 tablespoons white balsamic vinegar
1 teaspoon sugar
¼ teaspoon salt
¼ teaspoon ground black pepper

- In a small bowl, combine mayonnaise, vinegar, sugar, salt, and pepper, whisking well. Cover, and refrigerate until cold, at least 2 hours and up to a day.

"Tea! Bless ordinary everyday afternoon tea!"

—Agatha Christie

Pork Crostini with Corn-Avocado Relish
Yield: 24

2 (9- to 12-ounce) pork tenderloins
1 tablespoon plus 1 teaspoon olive oil, divided
½ teaspoon garlic salt
½ teaspoon chili powder
½ teaspoon smoked paprika
¼ teaspoon ground black pepper
1 recipe Crostini (recipe on page 135) or 24 prepared French bread crostini
1 recipe Corn-Avocado Relish (recipe follows)

- Preheat oven to 350°.
- Line a rimmed baking sheet with foil. Place tenderloins on pan. Drizzle evenly with 1 tablespoon olive oil. Season with garlic salt, chili powder, smoked paprika, and pepper, rubbing spices into pork.
- Bake for 20 minutes. Remove tenderloins from oven, and let rest for 15 minutes. (Pork will be rare.) Cut pork into ½-inch slices.
- In a medium nonstick sauté pan, heat remaining 1 teaspoon olive oil over medium-high heat. Add sliced pork, cooking on both sides until pork is no longer pink and is slightly charred, 1 to 2 minutes. Transfer to a plate, and cover to keep warm.
- Place 1 pork slice on each crostini. Top with Corn-Avocado Relish.
- Serve immediately.

Make-Ahead Tip: Pork tenderloins can be baked a day in advance. Wrap in foil, and refrigerate until needed. Let pork come to room temperature before continuing with recipe.

Corn-Avocado Relish
Gluten-free | Yield: 1 cup

½ cup diced ripe avocado
½ cup cooked fresh yellow corn
2 tablespoons minced red onion
2 tablespoons finely chopped orange bell pepper
2 tablespoons fresh lime juice
1 tablespoon canned minced pickled jalapeño pepper
1 tablespoon olive oil
¼ teaspoon salt
⅛ teaspoon ground black pepper

- In a medium bowl, combine avocado, corn, onion, bell pepper, lime juice, jalapeño pepper, olive oil, salt, and black pepper, tossing to blend. Use immediately.

Broccoli Salad Roulades

Pork Crostini with Corn-Avocado Relish

Flowery Pimiento Cheese
Tea Sandwiches

Flowery Pimiento Cheese Tea Sandwiches

Yield: 12

1 (8-ounce) block extra-sharp Cheddar cheese, coarsely shredded
¼ cup diced pimientos
⅓ cup mayonnaise
¼ teaspoon ground black pepper
24 slices whole-wheat bread, frozen

- In a medium bowl, combine cheese and pimientos, stirring well.
- In a small bowl, combine mayonnaise and pepper, whisking well. Add to cheese mixture, stirring to incorporate.
- Using a 2½-inch flower cutter, cut 24 shapes from frozen bread slices, discarding scraps. Spread 1 tablespoon cheese mixture each onto 12 bread flowers.
- Using a 1-inch round cutter, cut out centers from remaining 12 bread flowers, discarding centers. Place each atop a cheese-covered flower, aligning edges. Cover with damp paper towels, and let bread thaw completely (approximately 30 minutes) before serving.

Make-Ahead Tip: Pimiento cheese mixture can be made up to 3 days ahead and stored in an airtight container in the refrigerator.

Tarragon-Shrimp-Salad Finger Sandwiches

Yield: 12

4 cups water
3 slices lemon
2 (4-inch) sprigs fresh tarragon
¾ teaspoon salt, divided
½ teaspoon whole green peppercorns
1 pound medium frozen shrimp, thawed, peeled, and deveined
½ cup mayonnaise
1 tablespoon minced fresh tarragon
2 teaspoons fresh lemon juice
2 teaspoons fresh lime juice
1 teaspoon minced celery
1 teaspoon minced shallot
⅛ teaspoon ground black pepper
12 slices very thin white sandwich bread
Garnish: fresh tarragon sprigs

Tarragon-Shrimp-Salad Finger Sandwiches

- In a medium saucepan, combine water, lemon slices, tarragon sprigs, ½ teaspoon salt, and peppercorns, and bring to a boil. When mixture just comes to a boil, immediately remove saucepan from heat, add shrimp, and cover. Let stand for 5 minutes. Remove shrimp from poaching liquid, and place in a bowl filled with ice. Let cool.
- In a medium bowl, combine mayonnaise, minced tarragon, lemon juice, lime juice, celery, shallot, remaining ¼ teaspoon salt, and pepper, whisking to blend.
- Remove shrimp from ice, and blot dry with paper towels. Chop very finely. Add to mayonnaise mixture, stirring until combined. Place shrimp mixture in a covered container, and refrigerate until very cold, approximately 4 hours.
- Spread 2 tablespoons shrimp salad onto a bread slice. Top with another bread slice, and spread with another 2 tablespoons shrimp salad. Top with a third bread slice to make a triple-stack sandwich. Repeat with remaining bread slices and shrimp salad.
- Using a serrated knife in a gentle sawing motion, cut and discard crusts from all sides of bread. Cut 3 rectangular finger sandwiches from each sandwich.
- Serve immediately, or cover with damp paper towels, place in a covered container, and refrigerate for a few hours until serving time.
- Garnish each tea sandwich with a fresh tarragon sprig, if desired.

Green Grape and Kiwi Chicken Salad Sandwiches

Green Grape and Kiwi Chicken Salad Sandwiches
Yield: 6

2 cups chopped, cooked chicken breast
½ cup green grape halves
½ cup chopped kiwi
¼ cup diced celery
¼ cup slivered almonds, toasted
½ cup mayonnaise
1 tablespoon fresh lemon juice
¼ teaspoon salt
⅛ teaspoon ground black pepper
6 small leaves lettuce
6 small croissants, sliced horizontally

• In a medium bowl, combine chicken, grapes, kiwi, celery, and almonds.
• In a small bowl, combine mayonnaise, lemon juice, salt, and pepper, whisking well. Add to chicken mixture, stirring until combined. Cover, and refrigerate until cold, approximately 4 hours.
• Just before serving, place a lettuce leaf in each croissant, and divide chicken salad evenly among croissants.

Shrimp Salad Crostini

Shrimp Salad Crostini
Yield: 24

4 cups water
¼ cup rice vinegar
1 tablespoon Creole seasoning
1 pound small/medium shrimp, peeled and deveined
½ cup mayonnaise
2 teaspoons fresh lemon juice
1½ teaspoons hot pepper sauce
¼ teaspoon salt
¼ teaspoon ground black pepper
3 tablespoons finely chopped celery
1 tablespoon finely minced parsley
1 recipe Crostini (recipe follows) or 24 prepared French bread crostini
Garnish: fresh parsley leaves

• In a medium saucepan, combine water, rice vinegar, and Creole seasoning. Bring to a boil over high heat. When mixture just comes to a boil, immediately remove saucepan from heat, add shrimp, and cover. Let stand for 5 minutes. Remove shrimp from poaching liquid, and place in a bowl filled with ice. Let cool.
• In a small bowl, combine mayonnaise, lemon juice, hot sauce, salt, and pepper, whisking until smooth and creamy.
• Finely chop cooled shrimp, and place in a medium bowl. Add celery and parsley, tossing to combine. Add mayonnaise mixture to shrimp mixture, stirring until incorporated. Cover, and refrigerate for at least 4 hours and up to 8 hours.
• No more than 30 minutes before serving, divide shrimp salad among crostini.
• Garnish each canapé with a fresh parsley leaf, if desired.

Crostini
Yield: 24

2 tablespoons salted butter, softened
24 (¼-inch-thick) slices French bread

• Preheat oven to 350°.
• Spread butter onto each bread slice. Place slices, butter sides up, on a rimmed baking sheet.
• Bake until crisp and light golden brown, approximately 5 minutes. Let cool completely.
• Store crostini in an airtight container for up to a day.

Avocado-Tomatillo Crostini

> *"There is no trouble so great or grave that cannot be much diminished by a nice cup of tea."*
>
> —Bernard-Paul Heroux

- Remove and discard skins from tomatillos, reserving pulp. Press pulp from garlic cloves, discarding skins. Combine garlic pulp with tomatillo pulp, stirring until blended.
- In a medium bowl, combine ½ cup tomatillo mixture, avocado, onion, 1 tablespoon lime juice, cumin, and salt, stirring gently. (Add remaining 1 tablespoon lime juice if a stronger lime flavor is desired.)
- Spoon approximately 1 tablespoon avocado mixture onto each crostini.
- Garnish with red bell pepper strips, if desired.

*To caramelize onions, heat 2 teaspoons butter in a sauté pan over low heat. Add ¼ cup chopped onion, and cook, stirring occasionally, until onion is tender and slightly browned, 10 to 15 minutes.

Mini Dill Havarti and Turkey Panini
Yield: 16

½ cup mayonnaise
1 tablespoon fresh lemon juice
⅛ teaspoon ground black pepper
16 slices sourdough French sandwich bread
16 slices deli roast turkey
16 slices deli dill Havarti cheese
2 tablespoons salted butter, softened
16 slices cherry tomatoes
16 sprigs fresh dill

- In a small bowl, combine mayonnaise, lemon juice, and pepper, whisking well. Cover, and refrigerate aïoli until ready to use.
- Using a 2¼-inch square cutter, cut 32 squares from bread slices.
- Spread each bread square with ½ teaspoon aïoli.
- Trim turkey and cheese slices to fit bread squares, and place between 2 bread slices (aïoli sides to the inside). Spread outside of each bread slice with butter.
- Heat a nonstick griddle over medium-high heat.
- Grill each sandwich, pressing down lightly with a spatula to flatten slightly. Cook until golden brown, approximately 3 minutes per side.
- Top each sandwich with a cherry tomato slice and a dill sprig.
- Serve immediately.

Avocado-Tomatillo Crostini
Yield: 24

8 tomatillos, outer husks removed
2 cloves garlic, unpeeled
1 tablespoon olive oil
2 cups diced ripe avocado (approximately 2 avocados)
¼ cup caramelized onion*
1 to 2 tablespoons fresh lime juice
¼ teaspoon ground cumin
¼ teaspoon salt
1 recipe Crostini (recipe on page 135) or 24 prepared French bread crostini
Garnish: red bell pepper strips

- Preheat oven to 400°.
- Line a rimmed baking sheet with parchment paper.
- In a medium bowl, combine tomatillos, garlic, and olive oil, tossing to coat. Spread in a single layer on prepared baking sheet.
- Bake until tomatillos are completely soft, approximately 30 minutes. Let cool to room temperature.

Mini Dill Havarti and Turkey Panini

Mini Salmon Croquette Canapés

Mini Salmon Croquette Canapés
Yield: 20

1 (14.75-ounce) can pink salmon, drained and bones and skin removed
1⅓ cups panko (Japanese bread crumbs), divided
2 large eggs
1 tablespoon fresh lemon juice
1 teaspoon dried dill
¼ teaspoon salt
¼ teaspoon ground black pepper
¼ cup vegetable oil
20 leaves spring-mix lettuces
20 prepared French bread crostini or 1 recipe Crostini (recipe on page 135)
1 recipe Citrus Aïoli (recipe follows)
Garnish: fresh dill

- In a medium bowl, combine salmon, ⅓ cup panko, eggs, lemon juice, dill, salt, and pepper, stirring until well blended.
- Divide salmon mixture into 20 equal portions. Shape each portion into a 1½-inch croquette, and coat with remaining 1 cup panko. Flatten croquettes slightly.
- In a large nonstick sauté pan, heat oil over medium-high heat. Add croquettes to pan, and cook until golden brown, 3 to 4 minutes per side (longer if croquettes have been refrigerated). Drain on paper towels.
- Place a lettuce leaf on each crostini, and top with a croquette and a dollop of Citrus Aïoli.
- Garnish each canapé with fresh dill, if desired.

Make-Ahead Tip: Croquettes may be prepared a day in advance and refrigerated until ready to cook.

Citrus Aïoli
Gluten-free | *Yield: ½ cup*

½ cup mayonnaise
½ teaspoon fresh lemon zest
½ teaspoon fresh lime zest
1 teaspoon fresh lemon juice
1 teaspoon fresh lime juice
1 pinch salt

- In a small bowl, combine mayonnaise, zests, juices, and salt, whisking until combined. Cover, and refrigerate until needed, up to a day.

Buffalo Chicken and Slaw Canapés

Buffalo Chicken and Slaw Canapés
Yield: 16

2 tablespoons mayonnaise
2 teaspoons fresh lime juice
¼ teaspoon sugar
⅛ teaspoon salt
⅛ teaspoon ground black pepper
⅓ cup very finely chopped green cabbage
⅓ cup very finely chopped purple cabbage
¼ cup very finely chopped carrot
1 tablespoon very finely chopped green onion
8 slices sourdough sandwich bread, frozen
2 tablespoons salted butter, softened
16 thin slices deli buffalo chicken
Garnish: green onion slices

- In a large bowl, combine mayonnaise, lime juice, sugar, salt, and pepper, whisking until blended. Add cabbages, carrot, and green onion, stirring to combine. Cover, and refrigerate until needed, up to a day.
- Using a 2¼-inch round cutter, cut 16 rounds from frozen bread slices, discarding crusts. Cover with damp paper towels, and let bread thaw slightly (approximately 15 minutes).
- Spread each bread round with softened butter.
- In a large nonstick sauté pan, toast bread rounds over high heat until crisp and brown, approximately 1 minute per side, beginning with buttered side. Let cool slightly.
- Arrange a chicken slice on buttered side of each bread round, ruffling to fit. Top with slaw.
- Garnish each canapé with green onion slices, if desired.
- Serve immediately.

Reuben Canapés
Yield: 24

12 slices rye bread, frozen
24 thin slices Swiss cheese
½ cup mayonnaise
3 tablespoons ketchup
1 teaspoon Worcestershire sauce
½ teaspoon prepared horseradish
30 very thin slices deli corned beef
1½ cups sauerkraut, well drained
Garnish: corned beef rosettes*

- Preheat broiler.
- Using a 2¼-inch round cutter, cut 24 rounds from frozen bread slices, discarding crusts. Cover with damp paper towels, and let bread thaw slightly (approximately 15 minutes).
- Using the same cutter, cut 24 rounds from cheese slices.
- Heat a nonstick sauté pan over medium-high heat. Place bread rounds in pan, and toast on each side until golden brown, 2 to 3 minutes.
- In a small bowl, combine mayonnaise, ketchup, Worcestershire sauce, and horseradish, whisking well. Spread ½ teaspoon mayonnaise mixture onto each toasted bread round. Arrange a corned beef slice on each bread round, ruffling to fit. Top each with a cheese round.
- Place canapés on a broiler pan. Broil just until cheese melts, 1 to 2 minutes.
- Divide sauerkraut evenly among canapés.
- Garnish each canapé with a corned beef rosette, if desired.
- Serve immediately.

*Roll 2x¼-inch pieces of corned beef into cylinders, flaring out edges to create rosettes.

Roasted Vegetable–Cream Cheese Tea Sandwiches
Yield: 18

1 cup ¼-inch carrot slices
1 cup ¼-inch parsnip slices
1 cup chopped (1-inch squares) red bell pepper
1 cup chopped (1-inch squares) yellow bell pepper
1 cup ¼-inch sweet onion slices
1 tablespoon olive oil
1 teaspoon herbes de Provence
1 teaspoon salt
¼ teaspoon ground black pepper
1 (8-ounce) package cream cheese, softened
9 slices whole-wheat bread

- Preheat oven to 425°.
- Line a baking sheet with foil.
- In a large bowl, combine vegetables, olive oil, herbes de Provence, salt, and black pepper, tossing until well coated. Spread in a single layer on prepared baking sheet.
- Bake until vegetables are tender, 30 to 35 minutes. Let cool slightly. Chop finely.
- In a medium bowl, combine cream cheese and roasted vegetables, stirring well.
- Spread cream cheese mixture onto a bread slice. Top with another bread slice, and spread with cream cheese mixture. Top with a third bread slice to make a triple-stack sandwich. Repeat with remaining bread slices and cream cheese mixture.
- Using a serrated bread knife in a gentle sawing motion, trim and discard crusts from sandwiches. Cut each sandwich into 6 finger sandwiches.
- Serve immediately, or cover with damp paper towels, place in a covered container, and refrigerate for a few hours until serving time.

Make-Ahead Tip: *Cream cheese mixture can be made a day in advance and refrigerated in a covered container until needed. Let come to room temperature before using.*

"It is the personal choices and individual creative touches to the tiered stand that make teatime such a timeless pleasure."

—Jane Pettigrew

Reuben Canapés

Roasted Vegetable–Cream Cheese Tea Sandwiches

Caper-Celery Egg Salad Tea Sandwiches

Caper-Celery Egg Salad Tea Sandwiches
Yield: 12

6 large hard-boiled eggs, peeled
3 tablespoons mayonnaise
2 tablespoons whole-grain Dijon-style mustard
2 tablespoons finely chopped celery
1 tablespoon chopped capers
¼ teaspoon ground black pepper
12 slices seedless rye bread, frozen
Garnish: whole capers, baby arugula leaves

• In a medium bowl and using a pastry blender, chop eggs into small pieces. Add mayonnaise, mustard, celery, capers, and pepper, stirring until blended. Cover, and refrigerate until cold, approximately 4 hours.
• Using a 1¾-inch round cutter, cut 24 rounds from frozen bread slices, discarding scraps.
• Divide egg salad evenly among 12 bread rounds. Top with remaining bread rounds. Cover with damp paper towels, and let bread thaw completely (approximately 30 minutes) before serving.
• Garnish each tea sandwich with capers and baby arugula, if desired.

Italian BLT Tea Sandwiches
Yield: 12

6 slices soft Italian sandwich bread, frozen
1 (24-ounce) jar whole roasted red peppers
12 slices pancetta*
1 teaspoon olive oil
1 eggplant†, peeled and cut into 12 (¼-inch) slices
⅛ teaspoon garlic salt
⅛ teaspoon ground black pepper
¼ cup water
1 recipe Lemon-Oregano Aïoli (recipe follows)
12 leaves green leaf lettuce
12 slices Campari tomato
Garnish: fresh oregano sprigs, frilled picks

• Using a 2½-inch round cutter, cut 24 rounds from frozen bread slices, discarding scraps. Cover with damp paper towels, or store in a resealable plastic bag to keep from drying out while preparing other ingredients.
• Using the same cutter, cut 12 rounds from roasted red peppers. Drain on paper towels.
• In a large nonstick sauté pan, cook pancetta over medium-high heat until crisp, 3 to 4 minutes, turning halfway through cooking. Drain on paper towels.
• In the same pan, heat olive oil over medium-high heat.
• Sprinkle eggplant slices with garlic salt and pepper. Sear in hot pan for 1 to 2 minutes, add ¼ cup water, and cover pan with lid. Reduce heat to medium-low. Cook for 3 to 4 minutes, turning halfway through cooking, until eggplant is tender when pierced with a fork. Set eggplant aside.
• Spread Lemon-Oregano Aïoli onto each bread round. Using 12 bread rounds (aïoli sides up) as a base, assemble 12 sandwiches, stacking ingredients in the following order: lettuce, tomato, eggplant, red pepper round, pancetta, and another bread round (aïoli side down). Cover with damp paper towels, and let bread thaw completely (approximately 30 minutes) before serving.
• Garnish each tea sandwich with an oregano sprig and a frilled pick, if desired.

*Pancetta is an Italian bacon that is cut in round slices and can be found in the deli of most grocery stores.

†Choose an eggplant approximately 2½ inches in diameter.

Italian BLT Tea Sandwiches

Lemon-Oregano Aïoli
Gluten-free | *Yield: ½ cup*

½ cup mayonnaise
1 teaspoon minced fresh oregano
½ teaspoon fresh lemon zest
⅛ teaspoon salt
⅛ teaspoon ground black pepper

• In a small bowl, combine mayonnaise, oregano, lemon zest, salt, and pepper, stirring to blend. Cover, and refrigerate until needed, up to 2 days.

Avocado-Egg Salad Canapés

"Let us be grateful to people who make us happy, they are the charming gardeners who make our souls blossom."

—Marcel Proust

Herb and Flower Canapés

Avocado-Egg Salad Canapés
Yield: 48

8 hard-boiled eggs, peeled
⅓ cup mayonnaise
3 tablespoons Dijon-style mustard
3 tablespoons finely chopped fresh dill
¼ teaspoon salt
9 slices pumpernickel sandwich bread, frozen
3 avocados
1 whole lemon, cut into quarters
Garnish: fresh dill sprigs

• In a medium bowl and using a pastry blender, chop eggs into small pieces. Add mayonnaise, mustard, dill, and salt, stirring to blend. Cover, and refrigerate until cold, approximately 4 hours.
• Preheat oven to 350°.
• Line a rimmed baking sheet with parchment paper. Set aside.
• Using a 1½-inch scalloped-edge round cutter, cut 48 rounds from bread slices, discarding scraps. Place bread in a single layer on prepared baking sheet. Cover with damp paper towels, and let bread thaw slightly (approximately 15 minutes) before toasting.
• Remove paper towels, and bake for 10 minutes. Let cool completely, and store in a resealable plastic bag until needed.
• Peel whole avocadoes, and cut into thin vertical slices. Squeeze lemon juice over slices to prevent browning. Using the same cutter as for bread, cut 48 rounds from avocado slices.
• Place an avocado slice on top of each toasted bread round. Using a levered 2-teaspoon scoop, place egg salad on top of avocado rounds.
• Garnish with dill sprigs, if desired.
• Serve immediately, or refrigerate, lightly covered, for up to 30 minutes before serving.

Make-Ahead Tip: Bread rounds can be made earlier in the day and stored in an airtight container at room temperature until needed.

Herb and Flower Canapés
Yield: 16

4 slices pumpernickel bread, frozen
4 ounces cream cheese, softened
1 tablespoon fresh lemon juice
⅛ teaspoon salt
Garnish: fresh herbs (such as chives, dill, rosemary, and thyme), edible flowers (such as rosemary and lavender)

• Using a 1½-inch hexagonal cutter, cut 16 shapes from frozen bread slices, discarding crusts. Cover with damp paper towels, and let bread thaw slightly (approximately 15 minutes).
• In a small bowl, combine cream cheese, lemon juice, and salt, stirring until blended. Transfer cream cheese mixture to a piping bag fitted with small round tip.* Pipe a small button of cream cheese onto each bread shape. Using a small offset spatula, smooth cream cheese surface.
• Arrange herbs and flowers on cream cheese layer.
• Serve immediately, or cover with slightly damp paper towels to prevent drying out, and refrigerate for 1 to 2 hours.

*As an alternative, use a resealable bag with the corner snipped off.

Vegan Veggie Roulades

Lemon-Oregano Vinaigrette
Gluten-free | Yield: ½ cup

¼ cup extra-virgin olive oil
¼ cup fresh lemon juice
2 teaspoons finely chopped fresh oregano leaves
1 teaspoon finely chopped shallot
½ teaspoon Dijon-style mustard
½ teaspoon sugar
¼ teaspoon salt
⅛ teaspoon ground black pepper

• In a small jar with a screw-top lid, combine olive oil, lemon juice, oregano, shallot, mustard, sugar, salt, and pepper. Shake vigorously until emulsified. Let vinaigrette stand at room temperature for 30 minutes to allow flavor to develop.
• Use immediately, or cover, and refrigerate until needed, up to 2 days.

Kitchen Tip: Dried oregano can be substituted for fresh oregano leaves, but decrease the amount by one-half, as the flavor of dried herbs is more intense than that of fresh herbs.

Vegan Veggie Roulades
Yield: 21 (1-inch) slices

¾ cup hummus
3 (9x7-inch) flatbreads
1 cup baby kale leaves
⅓ cup very thinly sliced radishes
⅓ cup very thinly sliced yellow squash
⅓ cup orange bell pepper strips
3 tablespoons golden raisins
3 tablespoons toasted sesame seeds
1 recipe Lemon-Oregano Vinaigrette (recipe follows)

• Spread ¼ cup hummus on each flatbread. Arrange kale on top of hummus in an even layer. Top with radishes, squash, and bell pepper strips. Sprinkle raisins and sesame seeds on top. Drizzle lightly with Lemon-Oregano Vinaigrette.
• Starting from short end of flatbreads, roll up each one firmly, encasing ingredients. Using a serrated bread knife, cut into 1-inch slices.

Make-Ahead Tip: Roulades can be made a couple of hours in advance, wrapped securely in plastic wrap, and refrigerated until needed. Slice just before serving.

Walnut-Fig Tea Sandwiches
Yield: 6

1 (8-ounce) package cream cheese, softened
⅓ cup finely chopped toasted walnuts
¼ cup finely chopped dried figs
1 teaspoon fresh thyme leaves
⅛ teaspoon ground black pepper
12 slices firm white sandwich bread, frozen
Garnish: fresh thyme sprigs

• In a medium bowl, combine cream cheese, walnuts, figs, thyme leaves, and pepper, stirring to blend. Spread mixture in a thick, even layer onto 6 frozen bread slices. Set aside.
• Using a 3x2-inch diamond-shaped cutter, cut shapes from remaining 6 frozen bread slices, discarding scraps. Set aside.
• Using the same cutter, cut 6 shapes from cream cheese–topped bread slices, discarding scraps. Top each with a plain bread diamond. Cover with damp paper towels, and let bread thaw completely (approximately 30 minutes) before serving.
• Garnish each tea sandwich with a thyme sprig, if desired.

Walnut-Fig Tea Sandwiches

Dilly Roast Beef Tea Sandwiches

Dilly Roast Beef Tea Sandwiches
Yield: 12

½ cup mayonnaise
2 tablespoons finely chopped fresh dill
2 tablespoons finely chopped fresh chives
2 tablespoons finely chopped fresh basil
1 tablespoon red wine vinegar
⅛ teaspoon salt
⅛ teaspoon ground black pepper
24 slices white sandwich bread, frozen
12 very thin slices deli-style roast beef
12 sprigs fresh dill
Garnish: additional fresh dill sprigs

- In a small bowl, combine mayonnaise, dill, chives, basil, vinegar, salt, and pepper. Cover, and refrigerate aïoli until ready to use.
- Using a 2½-inch triangular cutter, cut 24 shapes from frozen bread slices.
- Spread ½ teaspoon aïoli onto each bread triangle. Set aside.
- Fold roast beef slices in half, then in half again to create triangles. Arrange roast beef on top of 12 bread triangles (aïoli sides up). Tuck a dill sprig into center of roast beef. Top each sandwich with another bread triangle (aïoli side down). Cover with damp paper towels, and let bread thaw completely (approximately 30 minutes) before serving.
- Garnish each tea sandwich with a fresh dill sprig, if desired.

Kitchen Tip: *To keep fresh dill from wilting, soak in ice water for 10 minutes.*

Roast Beef Tea Sandwiches with Smoked Paprika–Lime Aïoli
Yield: 9

6 slices potato bread
1 recipe Smoked Paprika–Lime Aïoli (recipe follows)
½ cup baby arugula leaves
27 thin slices Campari tomato
9 ultrathin slices roast beef
Garnish: baby arugula leaves

- Using a serrated bread knife in a gentle sawing motion, cut 3 even rectangles from each bread slice, trimming and discarding crusts. Store in a resealable plastic bag, or cover with damp paper towels to prevent drying out.
- Spread ½ teaspoon aïoli onto each bread rectangle. Using 9 bread rectangles (aïoli sides up) as a base, assemble sandwiches, stacking ingredients in the following order: arugula, 3 tomato slices (shingled to fit), roast beef slice (folded in half and gathered to ruffle), and another bread rectangle (aïoli side down).
- Garnish each tea sandwich with an arugula leaf, if desired.

Roast Beef Tea Sandwiches with Smoked Paprika–Lime Aïoli

Smoked Paprika–Lime Aïoli
Gluten-free | Yield: ½ cup

½ cup mayonnaise
1 tablespoon finely chopped cilantro
1 teaspoon fresh lime zest
1 teaspoon fresh lime juice
1 teaspoon smoked paprika
½ teaspoon ground cumin

- In a small bowl, combine mayonnaise, cilantro, lime zest, lime juice, paprika, and cumin, stirring to blend. Cover, and refrigerate until needed, up to 2 days.

Bacon, Mushroom, and Caramelized Onion Tea Sandwiches

Nutty Carrot, Pineapple, and Ginger Tea Sandwiches

Bacon, Mushroom, and Caramelized Onion Tea Sandwiches
Yield: 12

1 cup sliced white button mushrooms
1 teaspoon olive oil
⅜ teaspoon salt, divided
¼ teaspoon ground black pepper, divided
1 tablespoon salted butter
1 cup sliced sweet onion
1 (8-ounce) package cream cheese, softened
1 tablespoon heavy whipping cream
¼ cup finely chopped cooked bacon
1 teaspoon fresh thyme leaves
6 large slices firm whole-wheat bread, frozen
Garnish: fresh thyme sprigs

- Preheat oven to 350°.
- Line a rimmed baking sheet with parchment paper.
- In a small bowl, toss mushrooms with olive oil, ⅛ teaspoon salt, and ⅛ teaspoon pepper to coat. Spread in a single layer on prepared pan.
- Bake until mushrooms are tender and release their juices, approximately 20 minutes. Let cool completely. Finely chop, and set aside.
- In a small nonstick sauté pan, melt butter over medium-high heat. Add onion, and reduce heat to medium-low, cooking and stirring occasionally until onion is tender and lightly caramelized, approximately 10 minutes. Let cool completely. Finely chop, and set aside.
- In a medium mixing bowl, combine cream cheese, cream, remaining ¼ teaspoon salt, and remaining ⅛ teaspoon pepper. Beat at medium-high speed with a mixer until well blended. Add roasted mushrooms, caramelized onions, bacon, and thyme leaves, stirring by hand to incorporate.
- Spread a thick layer of mushroom mixture onto 3 frozen bread slices. Top each with another frozen bread slice.
- Using a 2-inch scalloped-edge round cutter, cut 4 tea sandwiches from each whole sandwich, discarding scraps. Cover with damp paper towels, and let bread thaw completely (approximately 30 minutes) before serving.
- Garnish with a fresh thyme sprig, if desired.

Nutty Carrot, Pineapple, and Ginger Tea Sandwiches
Yield: 9

1 (8-ounce) package cream cheese, softened
½ teaspoon freshly grated ginger root
½ cup grated carrot (medium grate)
½ cup canned crushed pineapple, well drained
¼ cup chopped, roasted, salted macadamia nuts
9 very thin slices wheat bread
Garnish: carrot strips

- In a medium bowl, combine cream cheese, ginger, carrot, pineapple, and macadamia nuts, stirring until well blended.
- Spread cream cheese mixture onto a bread slice. Top with another bread slice, and spread with cream cheese mixture. Top with a third bread slice to make a triple-stack sandwich. Repeat with remaining bread slices and cream cheese mixture.
- Using a serrated bread knife in a gentle sawing motion, trim and discard crusts from sandwiches. Cut each sandwich into 3 finger sandwiches.
- Serve immediately, or cover with damp paper towels, place in a covered container, and refrigerate for a few hours until serving time.
- Garnish with a carrot strip, if desired.

Make-Ahead Tip: Cream cheese mixture can be made a day in advance and refrigerated in a covered container until needed. Let come to room temperature before using.

> *"A man's social rank is determined by the amount of bread he eats in a sandwich."*
>
> —F. Scott Fitzgerald

Cucumber-Pear Canapés

Cucumber-Pear Canapés
Yield: 12

1 English cucumber
3 ripe Bosc pears
1 lime, cut in half
1 recipe Cilantro-Lime Aïoli (recipe follows)
12 large round crackers
Garnish: fresh cilantro sprigs

• Trim ends from cucumber. Using a mandoline, cut 36 very thin slices from cucumber. Set aside.
• Using a paring knife, cut 36 very thin slices from pear. Squeeze lime juice over pear slices to prevent browning. Blot dry.
• Spread 1 teaspoon Cilantro-Lime Aïoli onto each cracker. Top with 3 cucumber slices in an overlapping circle. Fan 3 pear slices on top of cucumbers.
• Garnish each canapé with a cilantro sprig, if desired.
• Serve immediately.

> "It's always teatime somewhere."
> —Anonymous

Cilantro-Lime Aïoli
Gluten-free | Yield: ⅓ cup

⅓ cup mayonnaise
3 tablespoons finely chopped fresh cilantro
1 tablespoon fresh lime zest
1 teaspoon fresh lime juice
⅛ teaspoon salt
⅛ teaspoon pepper

• In a small bowl, combine mayonnaise, cilantro, lime zest, lime juice, salt, and pepper, stirring to blend. Cover, and refrigerate until needed, up to a day.

Gouda-Goat–Pimiento Cheese Canapés
Yield: 24

1½ cups whole roasted red peppers
8 ounces Gouda cheese, finely shredded
4 ounces goat cheese, at room temperature
¼ cup mayonnaise
½ teaspoon Worcestershire sauce
¼ teaspoon ground black pepper
¼ teaspoon hot pepper sauce
24 petits toasts
Garnish: parsley leaves

• Using a 1-inch linzer-type flower cutter, cut 24 shapes from whole roasted red peppers. Set aside.
• Chop and reserve 3 tablespoons red pepper scraps.
• In a medium bowl, combine Gouda cheese, goat cheese, mayonnaise, chopped red peppers, Worcestershire sauce, black pepper, and hot sauce, stirring to blend. Spread pimiento cheese onto toasts. Top each with a pepper flower.
• Garnish each canapé with a parsley leaf, if desired.

Make-Ahead Tip: Pepper cutouts can be made a day in advance, covered with liquid from roasted red pepper jar, and refrigerated in a covered container. Blot dry on paper towels just before using.

Gouda-Goat–Pimiento Cheese Canapés

Smoked Salmon Salad Canapés

Smoked Salmon Salad Canapés
Yield: 8

2 (3.75-ounce) cans smoked salmon fillets in oil, drained
2 tablespoons mayonnaise
2 tablespoons finely chopped celery
1 tablespoon finely chopped green onion (green parts only)
1 tablespoon fresh lemon juice
2 teaspoons creamy horseradish
⅛ teaspoon ground black pepper
8 rectangular crackers (mini croccantini)
Garnish: celery leaves, lemon zest curls

- In a medium bowl, flake salmon with a fork. Add mayonnaise, celery, green onion, lemon juice, horseradish, and pepper, stirring to blend. Cover, and refrigerate until cold, approximately 4 hours.
- Spread approximately 2 tablespoons salmon salad onto each cracker.
- Garnish each canapé with a celery leaf and a lemon curl, if desired.

Kitchen Tip: Make lemon curls before juicing lemons! Use a Microplane Ultimate Citrus Tool to create long strips of lemon peel. Wrap strips around a straw to curl. Snip curls to desired lengths.

Checkerboard Herbed Butter Tea Sandwiches

Checkerboard Herbed Butter Tea Sandwiches
Yield: 10 to 12

8 tablespoons salted butter, at room temperature
1 tablespoon red wine vinegar
1 tablespoon finely chopped fresh dill
1 tablespoon finely chopped fresh chives
2 teaspoons dried dill
4 slices pumpernickel bread
3 slices seedless rye bread

- In a small bowl, combine butter, vinegar, fresh dill, chives, and dried dill, stirring until well blended.
- Using a serrated bread knife in a gentle sawing motion, cut 10 (4x1-inch) rectangles from pumpernickel bread slices and 8 from rye bread slices, discarding scraps.
- On a work surface, arrange 3 bread rectangles, long sides together, alternating pumpernickel and rye. Spread a thick even layer of herbed butter onto bread layer, holding rectangles together with fingers. Place 3 more bread rectangles on top, alternating rye and pumpernickel. Spread another thick even layer of herbed butter onto bread layer. Place 3 more bread rectangles on top, alternating pumpernickel and rye. Repeat with remaining bread rectangles and butter. Wrap sandwiches in damp paper towels and plastic wrap, and refrigerate until set, approximately 2 hours.
- Just before serving, unwrap sandwiches. Using a serrated bread knife in a gentle sawing motion, trim and discard uneven ends from sandwiches. Cut each sandwich crossways into ½-inch slices.

Kitchen Tip: We used both fresh and dried dill in these sandwiches to impart a fresh, intense flavor. To chop herbs finely, use kitchen scissors.

Summertime Ham Sandwiches

Summertime Ham Sandwiches
Yield: 8

8 ciabatta rolls, baked according to package
    directions and cooled
1 recipe Sun-Dried Tomato Aïoli (recipe follows)
24 leaves spring-mix lettuces
8 slices deli ham
Garnish: decorative wooden picks

• Slice rolls in half horizontally. Spread Sun-Dried Tomato Aïoli evenly inside rolls. Arrange 3 lettuce leaves on bottom half of each roll. Arrange ham on top of lettuce leaves (ruffling to fit roll). Top with remaining halves of rolls (aïoli side down).
• Garnish each sandwich with a decorative pick, if desired.
• Serve immediately.

Sun-Dried Tomato Aïoli
Gluten-free | *Yield: ½ cup*

2 tablespoons minced sun-dried tomato
1 cup boiling water
½ cup mayonnaise
1 teaspoon fresh lemon juice
¼ cup finely grated Parmesan cheese
1 teaspoon chopped fresh thyme
1 teaspoon chopped fresh oregano
¼ teaspoon salt
¼ teaspoon ground black pepper

• In a small bowl, combine sun-dried tomato and boiling water. Let stand for 1 minute to rehydrate. Drain and discard water.
• In another small bowl, combine sun-dried tomato, mayonnaise, lemon juice, Parmesan cheese, thyme, oregano, salt, and pepper, whisking well. Cover, and refrigerate until needed, up to 2 days.

Pickled Okra Roulades
Gluten-free variation | *Yield: 12 to 14 (1-inch) slices*

1 (24-ounce) jar mild pickled okra spears
½ cup spreadable cream cheese, divided
2 (9-inch) sun-dried-tomato flour tortillas*
6 to 8 thin slices deli smoked turkey breast

• Cut stem ends and tips from okra spears. Blot okra dry with paper towels. Set aside.
• Spread 2 tablespoons cream cheese over each tortilla. Place 3 or 4 turkey slices over cream cheese layer on each tortilla. Spread remaining 2 tablespoons cream cheese over turkey layer of each tortilla.
• Starting at end of tortilla closest to you, place a row of 3 okra spears. Make another row of okra spears next to the first row. Place a third row of okra spears on top of first 2 rows. Roll up tortilla away from you, pressing firmly to keep okra spears together. End with seam side down.
• Using a serrated knife, cut off ends of each rolled-up tortilla to make a neat cylinder approximately 6 to 7 inches long. Cut cylinders into 1-inch slices.

*To make a gluten-free version, replace flour tortillas with gluten-free garden vegetable–flavored wraps, such as Toufayan Bakeries.

Make-Ahead Tip: *Roulades can be made a couple of hours in advance, wrapped securely in plastic wrap, and refrigerated until needed. Cut into slices just before serving.*

Pickled Okra Poulades

Beef and Cheddar Triple-Stack Sandwiches
Yield: 8

2 (6-ounce) beef tenderloin fillets
1 tablespoon olive oil, divided
¼ teaspoon garlic salt
¼ teaspoon ground black pepper
¼ teaspoon ground half-sharp paprika*
1 teaspoon butter, cut in half
16 slices sourdough sandwich bread, frozen
8 slices hearty wheat sandwich bread, frozen
8 slices sharp Cheddar cheese
1 recipe Horseradish Aïoli (recipe follows)
½ cup baby arugula leaves
24 slices Campari tomatoes
Garnish: decorative picks

- Preheat oven to 350°.
- Line a rimmed baking sheet with foil.
- Rub each fillet with 1 teaspoon olive oil. Evenly season on all sides with garlic salt, pepper, and paprika, rubbing spices into filets. Let fillets sit at room temperature for 30 minutes.
- In a nonstick sauté pan, heat remaining 1 teaspoon olive oil over medium-high heat. Add meat to pan, and sear fillets on all sides until browned, 2 to 3 minutes per side. Transfer fillets to prepared baking sheet.
- Bake fillets until desired degree of doneness is reached†, 5 to 7 minutes for rare. Add more baking time for well done.
- When fillets are cooked, top each piece with ½ teaspoon butter. Wrap securely in foil. Let rest for at least 15 minutes.
- Using a 2½-inch round cutter, cut 16 rounds from frozen sourdough-bread slices and 8 rounds from frozen wheat-bread slices. Cover with damp paper towels, or store in a resealable plastic bag to keep from drying out while preparing other ingredients. Let thaw completely (approximately 30 minutes).
- Using the same cutter, cut 8 rounds from cheese slices.
- Fifteen minutes before serving, slice fillets into 4x¼-inch pieces.
- Spread Horseradish Aïoli onto each bread round. Using 8 sourdough bread rounds (aïoli sides up) as bases, assemble sandwiches, stacking ingredients in the following order: 2 fillet slices (ruffled to fit bread rounds), cheese, a wheat bread round (aïoli side up), arugula, tomato slices, and a sourdough round (aïoli side down).
- Garnish each tea sandwich with a decorative pick, if desired.
- Serve immediately.

*We used Penzeys Hungarian Style Half-Sharp Paprika, available at penzeys.com.

†The best way to ensure meat reaches a safe internal temperature is to use a meat thermometer. Beef should be cooked to at least 140° (rare).

Make-Ahead Tip: Prepare beef tenderloin fillets no more than a day ahead. Wrap tightly in foil, and refrigerate until needed. Cut into slices 15 minutes before serving.

Horseradish Aïoli
Gluten-free | Yield: ⅓ cup

⅓ cup mayonnaise
2 teaspoons prepared horseradish

- In a small bowl, combine mayonnaise and horseradish, whisking until smooth and creamy. Cover, and refrigerate until needed, up to 2 days.

"I shouldn't think even millionaires could eat anything nicer than new bread and real butter and honey for tea."

—Dodie Smith, *I Capture the Castle*

Sweets

Cakes AND Cupcakes

ITALIAN CREAM CUPCAKES
(recipe on page 176)

Petite Strawberry Jam Cakes

- Preheat oven to 350°.
- Line an 18x13-inch rimmed baking sheet with parchment paper, and spray with nonstick cooking spray.
- In a medium bowl, combine flour, baking powder, salt, and baking soda, whisking well.
- In a large mixing bowl, beat butter at high speed with an electric mixer until creamy. Add sugar, and beat until light and fluffy, approximately 4 minutes. Add jam. Add eggs, one at a time, beating well after each addition. Add vanilla extract and food coloring (to achieve desired color), beating to combine.
- With mixer on low speed, add flour mixture to butter mixture in thirds, alternately with buttermilk, beginning and ending with flour mixture. Beat until combined.
- Pour batter into prepared pan, and spread evenly. Tap pan several times on countertop to reduce air bubbles in batter.
- Bake on middle rack of oven until a wooden pick inserted in the center comes out clean, approximately 15 minutes.
- Let cake cool completely in pan on a wire rack. Freeze for 1 hour.
- Using a 2-inch round cutter, cut 34 circles from cake.
- Place Strawberry–Cream Cheese Frosting in a pastry bag fitted with a large open-star tip (Wilton #1M). Pipe frosting onto 17 cake circles. Refrigerate for 15 minutes.
- Top each cake circle with another cake circle, and pipe frosting onto top. Refrigerate for at least 15 minutes or until needed.
- Garnish each with a strawberry rosette just before serving, if desired.

Petite Strawberry Jam Cakes
Yield: 17

2 cups sifted cake flour
1 teaspoon baking powder
½ teaspoon salt
¼ teaspoon baking soda
½ cup salted butter, softened
1¼ cups sugar
½ cup seedless strawberry jam
3 large eggs
½ teaspoon vanilla extract
Red food coloring paste
⅓ cup whole buttermilk
1 recipe Strawberry–Cream Cheese Frosting (recipe follows)
Garnish: fresh strawberry rosettes*

Strawberry–Cream Cheese Frosting
Yield: 2½ cups

4 ounces cream cheese, softened
½ cup salted butter, softened
2 tablespoons seedless strawberry jam
½ teaspoon vanilla extract
3½ cups confectioners' sugar
Red food coloring paste (optional)

- In a large mixing bowl, combine cream cheese, butter, jam, vanilla extract, and confectioners' sugar. Beat at low speed with an electric mixer until incorporated. Increase speed to high, and beat until frosting is light and fluffy, 2 to 3 minutes.
- If desired, tint frosting with food coloring, beating until uniform.
- Refrigerate for 30 minutes before using.

STRAWBERRY ROSETTES how-to on page 235

Vanilla–Sour Cream Fairy Cakes
Yield: 39

½ cup salted butter, softened
1 cup castor sugar or superfine sugar
2 large eggs
1½ cups sifted cake flour
1½ teaspoons baking powder
⅛ teaspoon salt
¼ cup whole milk
¼ cup sour cream
1½ teaspoons vanilla extract
1 recipe Very Vanilla Buttercream (recipe follows)
Garnish: pearlescent sugar*

- Preheat oven to 350°.
- Line 39 wells of a 48-well mini cupcake pan† with paper liners.
- In a large mixing bowl, combine butter and sugar. Beat with a mixer at high speed until light and fluffy, 3 to 5 minutes. Add eggs, one at a time, beating well after each addition.
- In a medium bowl, combine flour, baking powder, and salt, whisking well.
- In a liquid-measuring cup, combine milk, sour cream, and vanilla extract, whisking well. Add flour mixture to butter mixture in thirds, alternately with milk mixture, beginning and ending with flour mixture.
- Using a levered 2-teaspoon scoop, drop batter into prepared wells of muffin pan.
- Bake until cupcakes are lightly browned and a wooden pick inserted in the centers comes out clean, 11 to 12 minutes. Let cupcakes cool completely on a wire cooling rack.
- Place Very Vanilla Buttercream in a piping bag fitted with a large open-star tip (Wilton #1M), and pipe a rosette on top of cupcakes. (Hold bag upright and pipe frosting downward.)
- Garnish with a sprinkle of pearlescent sugar, if desired.
- Refrigerate in a covered container until serving time.

*We used Cake Mate Cupcake Gems Pearlescent Sugar.

†We used a Wilton Perfect Results Mini Muffin Pan, which is available at wilton.com.

Vanilla–Sour Cream Fairy Cakes

Very Vanilla Buttercream
Yield: 3 cups

1 cup salted butter, softened
5 cups confectioners' sugar
2 tablespoons whole milk
1 tablespoon vanilla extract
¼ teaspoon salt

- In a large mixing bowl, combine butter, confectioners' sugar, milk, vanilla extract, and salt. Beat with a mixer at high speed until combined and fluffy.
- Use immediately.

Make-Ahead Tip: *Buttercream can be made a day in advance and refrigerated in a covered container until needed. Let come to room temperature, and beat with a mixer for 1 minute before piping.*

Coconut-Lime Cakes

- Preheat oven to 350°.
- Spray a 18x13-inch rimmed baking sheet with nonstick cooking spray. Line with parchment paper, and spray again.
- In a medium bowl, combine flour, lime zest, baking powder, baking soda, and salt, whisking well.
- In a large mixing bowl, beat butter at medium speed with an electric mixer until creamy. Gradually add sugar, beating until light and fluffy, approximately 3 minutes. Add eggs, one at a time, beating well after each addition. Add coconut extract and vanilla extract.
- Add flour mixture to butter mixture in thirds, alternately with buttermilk, beginning and ending with flour. Pour batter into prepared pan, and spread evenly. Tap pan sharply on countertop to reduce air bubbles.
- Bake until a wooden pick inserted in the center comes out clean, 15 to 16 minutes. Let cool in pan on a wire rack.
- When completely cool, remove from pan, and cut into 2 (13x9-inch) portions. Spread Lime Buttercream evenly over each portion. Stack 1 portion on top of the other. Freeze until firm, approximately 1 hour.
- Using a long, sharp knife and pressing downward, trim crusts from edges of frozen cake stack, and cut into 2½-inch squares.
- Garnish with chopped macadamias and toasted coconut.
- Let come to room temperature before serving, if desired.

Make-Ahead Tip: Cake can be baked in advance, frosted and assembled, wrapped securely in plastic wrap, and frozen for up to a week. Cut while frozen. Let thaw before garnishing and serving.

Coconut-Lime Cakes
Yield: 15 servings

2½ cups plus 5 tablespoons sifted cake flour
1 tablespoon fresh lime zest
2 teaspoons baking powder
½ teaspoon baking soda
½ teaspoon salt
1 cup salted butter, softened
1¾ cups sugar
4 large eggs
1½ teaspoons coconut extract
½ teaspoon vanilla extract
1 cup whole buttermilk
1 recipe Lime Buttercream (recipe follows)
Garnish: chopped roasted, salted macadamias and toasted, shredded sweetened coconut

Lime Buttercream
Yield: 2½ cups

1 cup butter, softened
4 cups confectioners' sugar
1 teaspoon fresh lime zest
2 tablespoons fresh lime juice

- In a large mixing bowl, combine butter, confectioners' sugar, lime zest, and lime juice. Beat at medium speed with an electric mixer, gradually increasing to high speed, until smooth and creamy.
- Use immediately.

Make-Ahead Tip: Lime Buttercream can be made a day in advance, covered, and refrigerated until needed. Let come to room temperature before spreading.

Almond-Apple Tea Bread
Yield: 3 mini loaves

½ cup superfine or castor sugar
½ cup all-purpose flour
½ cup ground slivered almonds
¼ teaspoon salt
4 large egg whites
½ cup salted butter, melted
½ cup diced peeled apple
¼ teaspoon apple pie spice
Garnish: confectioners' sugar

- Preheat oven to 350°.
- Spray 3 (6x3¼-inch) mini loaf pans with nonstick baking spray with flour.
- In a large bowl, combine sugar, flour, almonds, and salt, whisking well. Add egg whites, stirring until incorporated. Add melted butter, stirring well. Divide mixture evenly among prepared loaf pans. Sprinkle apples evenly over batter. Sprinkle apple pie spice evenly over apples.
- Bake loaves until tops are golden and a wooden pick inserted in the centers comes out clean, 40 to 43 minutes. Let cool in pans for 5 minutes. Remove from pans, and transfer to a wire rack. Let cool completely.
- Garnish with confectioners' sugar, if desired.

Make-Ahead Tip: These breads are best on the day they are made, but they will keep for a few days wrapped securely in plastic wrap.

Editor's Note: There is no leavening in this recipe. The loaves are dense yet moist and have a fine crumb.

Almond-Apple Tea Bread

Orange-Lavender Mini Cupcakes

- Using a levered 1-tablespoon scoop, drop batter into baking cups.
- Bake until a wooden pick inserted in the centers of cupcakes comes out clean, approximately 12 minutes. Let cool in pans for 5 minutes. Transfer to a wire rack, and let cool completely.
- Place Buttercream Frosting in a piping bag fitted with a medium open-star tip (Wilton #21). Pipe frosting onto cooled cupcakes.
- Refrigerate cupcakes, covered, until ready to serve.
- Garnish with lavender petals just before serving, if desired.

Make-Ahead Tip: Cupcakes can be made in advance and frozen (unfrosted) in an airtight container for up to a week. Let thaw before frosting.

Buttercream Frosting
Yield: 1½ cups

¾ cup salted butter, softened
2½ cups confectioners' sugar
2 tablespoons plus 2 teaspoons whole milk

- In a large mixing bowl, beat butter at high speed with an electric mixer until creamy. Add confectioners' sugar and milk, starting at low speed and gradually increasing to high speed. Beat until light and creamy.
- Use immediately.

Orange-Lavender Mini Cupcakes
Yield: 40

½ cup salted butter, softened
1 cup sugar
2 large eggs
¼ teaspoon orange extract
1½ cups all-purpose flour
1 tablespoon fresh orange zest
1½ teaspoons dried culinary lavender
½ teaspoon baking powder
¼ teaspoon salt
⅔ cup whole milk
1 recipe Buttercream Frosting (recipe follows)
Garnish: lavender petals

- Preheat oven to 350°.
- Line 40 wells of 2 (24-well) mini muffin pans with paper liners.
- In a large mixing bowl, beat butter at high speed with an electric mixer until creamy. Gradually add sugar, beating until light and fluffy, approximately 5 minutes. Add eggs, one at a time, beating well after each addition. Add orange extract, beating to combine.
- In a medium bowl, combine flour, orange zest, lavender, baking powder, and salt, whisking well. Add half of flour mixture to butter mixture, beating at low speed. Add milk and remaining flour mixture, beating to incorporate.

Peanut Butter Pound Cake
Yield: 12 to 16 servings

½ cup salted butter, softened
½ cup creamy peanut butter
1½ cups sugar
1¼ teaspoons vanilla extract
3 large eggs, at room temperature
1½ cups sifted cake flour
¼ teaspoon baking powder
¼ teaspoon salt
½ cup whole milk
1 recipe Peanut Butter Frosting (recipe follows)
Garnish: chopped peanuts

- Preheat oven to 350°.
- Spray a 6-cup Bundt pan* with nonstick baking spray with flour.
- In a large mixing bowl, beat butter at medium-high speed with an electric mixer until creamy. Add peanut butter, sugar, and vanilla extract, beating until light and fluffy, approximately 3 minutes. Add eggs, one at a time, beating well after each addition.
- In a medium bowl, combine flour, baking powder, and salt, whisking well. Add flour mixture to peanut-butter mixture in thirds, alternately with milk, beginning and ending with flour. Place batter in prepared pan, filling no more than three-quarters, and smooth evenly. Rap pan

168 The Ultimate TeaTime Collection | CAKES AND CUPCAKES

Peanut Butter Pound Cake

on the countertop several times to settle batter and reduce air bubbles.
- Bake until a wooden pick inserted near the center comes out clean, 53 to 55 minutes. (Cake will have a high dome but will not spill out of pan). Let cake cool in pan for 10 minutes. Using a long, serrated knife, trim dome off of cake so cake will sit level when inverted. Invert cake onto a wire rack, and let cool completely.
- Place Peanut Butter Frosting in a resealable plastic bag with a corner snipped off to make a small opening. Pipe frosting onto cooled cake in a decorative fashion.
- Garnish with chopped peanuts, if desired.

*We used NordicWare's 6-cup Anniversary Cast Bundt Pan, which is available at nordicware.com.

Peanut Butter Frosting
Yield: 1 cup

¼ cup creamy peanut butter
¼ cup light corn syrup
1 cup confectioners' sugar
2 teaspoons whole milk
½ teaspoon vanilla extract

- In a small saucepan, combine peanut butter and corn syrup. Cook over low heat, stirring until smooth and creamy. Remove from heat, and add confectioners' sugar, milk, and vanilla extract, stirring until incorporated.
- Use immediately.

Individual Chocolate-Banana Bundt Cakes
Yield: 10

2 ounces unsweetened baking chocolate
1 cups all-purpose flour
¼ teaspoon baking soda
⅛ teaspoon salt
½ cup salted butter, softened
¾ cup sugar
1 large egg
½ teaspoon vanilla extract
¼ cup whole buttermilk
⅓ cup mashed ripe banana
Garnish: confectioners' sugar

- Preheat oven to 325°.
- Spray 10 wells of 2 (6-well) swirled Bundt pans* with nonstick baking spray with flour.
- Melt chocolate according to package instructions.
- In a medium bowl, combine flour, baking soda, and salt, whisking well.
- In a large mixing bowl, combine butter and sugar. Beat at medium speed with an electric mixer until creamy, approximately 3 minutes. Add egg, beating well. Add vanilla extract, beating until bended. Add flour mixture to butter mixture in thirds, alternately with buttermilk, beginning and ending with flour mixture. Add banana and melted chocolate, beating just until incorporated.
- Using a levered ¼-cup scoop, divide batter evenly among prepared wells of pans. Tap pan forcefully on counter several times to settle batter and to remove air bubbles.
- Bake until a wooden pick inserted in the centers comes out clean, approximately 17 to 19 minutes. Let cool in pans for 10 minutes. Transfer to a wire rack, and let cool completely.
- Garnish with a dusting of confectioners' sugar before serving, if desired.

*We used a Nordicware Anniversary Bundtlette Pan, which is available at nordicware.com.

Individual Chocolate-Banana Bundt Cakes

Red Velvet Mini Cupcakes
Yield: 48

1¼ cups sifted cake flour
1 tablespoon plus 2 teaspoons natural unsweetened cocoa powder
¼ teaspoon baking powder
¼ teaspoon salt
¼ cup salted butter, softened
¾ cup sugar
1 large egg
1 teaspoon vanilla extract
½ cup whole buttermilk
1 tablespoon liquid red food coloring
½ teaspoon white vinegar
½ teaspoon baking soda
1 recipe Vanilla Buttercream (recipe follows)
Garnish: White Chocolate Hearts and red sprinkles (nonpareils)

- Preheat oven to 350°.
- Line 2 (24-well) mini muffin pans with cupcake liners.
- In a medium bowl, combine flour, cocoa powder, baking powder, and salt, whisking well.
- In a large mixing bowl, beat butter at medium speed with an electric mixer until soft and creamy, approximately 1 minute. Gradually add sugar, beating at high speed until light and fluffy, approximately 3 minutes. Add egg, beating until incorporated. Add vanilla extract, beating until incorporated.
- In a liquid measuring cup, combine buttermilk and red food coloring, whisking to blend. Add flour mixture to butter mixture in thirds, alternately with buttermilk mixture, beginning and ending with flour mixture. Beat until incorporated.
- In a small bowl, combine vinegar and baking soda, stirring until mixture fizzes. Quickly add mixture to cake batter, beating at low speed just until incorporated. Working quickly and using a levered 2-teaspoon scoop, divide batter evenly among wells of prepared muffin pans.
- Bake until a wooden pick inserted in the centers comes out clean, 13 to 14 minutes. Let cupcakes cool in pans for 5 minutes. Transfer to a wire rack, and let cool completely.
- Place Vanilla Buttercream in a piping bag fitted with a large open-star tip (Wilton #1). Pipe a decorative swirl on tops of cupcakes.
- Store, covered, in the refrigerator until serving time.
- Just before serving, garnish each cupcake with a White Chocolate Heart and red sprinkles, if desired.

Vanilla Buttercream
Yield: 2½ cups

1 cup salted butter, softened
4 cups confectioners' sugar
3 tablespoons whole milk
½ teaspoon vanilla extract

Red Velvet Mini Cupcakes

- In a large mixing bowl, combine butter, confectioners' sugar, milk, and vanilla extract. Beat with an electric mixer, starting at low speed and gradually increasing to high speed, until smooth and creamy.
- Use immediately.

White Chocolate Hearts
Yield: 48 hearts

1½ (4-ounce) bars white chocolate
Red sprinkles (nonpareils)

- Line a rimmed baking sheet with waxed paper. Set aside.
- Melt white chocolate according to package directions. Working quickly and using an offset spatula, spread melted chocolate onto prepared baking sheet in an even layer approximately ¼ inch thick. Evenly distribute sprinkles over melted chocolate. Refrigerate until chocolate is firm, approximately 1 hour.
- Using a 1-inch heart-shaped cutter*, cut shapes from chilled chocolate. Refrigerate until needed.

*We used a heart-shaped linzer cutter.

> *"Whence could it have come to me, this all-powerful joy? I was conscious that it was connected with the taste of the tea and the cake . . ."*
>
> —Marcel Proust,
> *Remembrance of Things Past*

White Chocolate–Lemon Cake
Yield: 24 servings

1 (15.25-ounce) white cake mix
3 large eggs
1 cup water
¼ cup vegetable oil
⅓ cup sour cream
1 tablespoon fresh lemon zest
1 recipe Lemon-Mascarpone Filling (recipe follows)
1 recipe Lemon–White Chocolate Buttercream (recipe follows)
Garnish: lemon curls and fresh mint

- Preheat oven to 350°.
- Spray an 18x13-inch rimmed baking sheet with nonstick cooking spray. Line with parchment paper, and spray again. Set aside.
- In a large mixing bowl, combine cake mix, eggs, water, oil, sour cream, and lemon zest. Beat at low speed with an electric mixer for 30 seconds, scraping down sides of bowl as necessary. Increase speed to medium, and beat for 2 minutes. Spread batter into prepared pan.
- Bake until light golden brown and a wooden pick inserted in the center comes out clean, 11 to 13 minutes. Let cake cool completely in pan on a wire rack.
- Remove cake from pan, and place on a cutting surface. Cut cake into 2 (13x9-inch) portions. Spread Lemon-Mascarpone Filling on one portion. Top with remaining cake portion. Spread top with Lemon–White Chocolate Buttercream. Using a sharp serrated knife, trim sides of cake, discarding crusts. Cut into 2½-x-1-inch pieces.
- Store cakes in a covered container in the refrigerator.
- Garnish with lemon curls and fresh mint just before serving, if desired.

Kitchen Tip: *To make cake easier to cut, place in freezer for approximately 30 minutes.*

Lemon-Mascarpone Filling
Yield: 2 cups

1 (10-ounce) jar lemon curd
1 (8-ounce) carton mascarpone cheese

- In a small bowl, stir lemon curd vigorously to loosen. Add mascarpone cheese, stirring until combined. Use immediately, or refrigerate in a covered container until needed.

Lemon–White Chocolate Buttercream
Yield: 3 cups

1 cup salted butter, softened
3½ cups confectioners' sugar
1 teaspoon fresh lemon zest
2 tablespoons fresh lemon juice
½ teaspoon lemon extract
½ teaspoon salt
1 (4-ounce) bar white chocolate, melted and cooled

- In a large mixing bowl, combine butter, confectioners' sugar, lemon zest, lemon juice, lemon extract, and salt. Beat with an electric mixer, starting at low speed and gradually increasing to high speed. Add white chocolate, beating until incorporated.
- Use immediately, or refrigerate in a covered container until needed. Let come to room temperature to soften, and beat with an electric mixer for 1 minute before using.

White Chocolate–Lemon Cake

Flourless Hazelnut Torte with Apricot Preserves

Flourless Hazelnut Torte with Apricot Preserves

Gluten-free | Yield: 12 to 14 servings

1¼ cups whole raw hazelnuts with skins
4 large eggs, separated
¾ cup superfine or castor sugar
¼ teaspoon vanilla extract
¼ teaspoon salt
1 (10-ounce) jar apricot preserves

- Preheat oven to 350°.
- Spray a 9-inch round springform pan with nonstick cooking spray. Set aside.
- In the work bowl of a food processor, pulse hazelnuts until finely ground, being careful not to overprocess into a nut butter. Set aside.
- In a large mixing bowl, combine egg yolks and sugar. Beat at high speed with an electric mixer until light and creamy, approximately 2 minutes. Add vanilla extract, stirring to combine. Set aside.
- Add salt to hazelnuts, whisking well. Add hazelnut mixture to egg yolk mixture, beating at medium speed until incorporated. (Batter will be very stiff.) Set aside.
- In another mixing bowl, beat egg whites at high speed with an electric mixer until stiff peaks form. Spoon one-third of beaten egg whites into hazelnut batter, stirring vigorously to loosen mixture. Add remaining egg whites, folding to incorporate. Spread mixture into prepared pan, smoothing with an offset spatula.
- Bake until torte is golden brown and a wooden pick inserted in the center comes out clean, 27 to 29 minutes. (Top of torte should feel somewhat firm to the touch, and edges should be golden brown.) Let torte cool completely in pan, approximately 1 hour.
- Using a sharp knife or a thin offset spatula, loosen sides of torte from pan before removing sides of pan. In the same manner, loosen torte from bottom of pan. Place torte on a cake plate.
- In a small saucepan, melt apricot preserves over low heat, stirring to loosen. Spoon preserves over surface of torte, spreading evenly.

Make-Ahead Tip: Flourless Hazelnut Torte can be made in advance, wrapped tightly in plastic wrap, and frozen for up to 1 week. Let thaw before spreading apricot preserves over torte.

Spiced Plum Bundt Cake

Yield: 12 to 16 servings

½ cup chopped dried plums
1 cup salted butter, softened
1 cup sugar
3 large eggs, at room temperature
½ teaspoon vanilla extract
2 cups sifted cake flour
1 teaspoon ground cinnamon
¼ teaspoon baking soda

Spiced Plum Bundt Cake

¼ teaspoon salt
½ cup sour cream
⅓ cup chopped toasted walnuts
Garnish: confectioners' sugar

- Preheat oven to 325°.
- Spray a 6-cup Bundt pan* with nonstick baking spray with flour.
- Place dried plums in a small bowl, and cover with very hot water. Let stand for 5 minutes to rehydrate. Drain well.
- In a large mixing bowl, beat butter at high speed with an electric mixer until creamy. Add sugar, beating until light and fluffy, approximately 5 minutes. Add eggs, one at a time, beating well after each addition. Add vanilla extract, beating until incorporated.
- In a medium bowl, combine cake flour, cinnamon, baking soda, and salt, whisking well. With mixer at low speed, add flour mixture to butter mixture in thirds, alternately with sour cream, beginning and ending with flour mixture. Add rehydrated plums and walnuts, stirring to combine. (Batter will be thick.) Place batter in prepared pan, filling no more than three-quarters, and spread evenly. Smooth top with a spatula, and tap cake pan firmly on countertop several times to settle batter and reduce air bubbles.
- Bake until a wooden pick inserted in the center comes out clean, 50 to 52 minutes. Let cake cool in pan for 10 minutes. Using a long, serrated knife, trim dome off of cake so cake will sit level when inverted. Invert cake onto a wire rack, and let cool completely.
- Garnish with a dusting of confectioners' sugar, if desired.

*We used Nordicware's 6-cup Anniversary Cast Bundt Pan, which is available at nordicware.com.

Make-Ahead Tip: Cake can be baked in advance, wrapped securely in plastic wrap, and frozen (ungarnished) for up to a week. Let cake thaw completely before garnishing with confectioners' sugar.

Italian Cream Cupcakes

Italian Cream Cupcakes
Yield: 17

½ cup salted butter, softened
1 cup sugar
2 large eggs
¼ cup sour cream
¼ cup whole milk
1 teaspoon vanilla extract
1½ cups sifted cake flour
1½ teaspoons baking powder
⅛ teaspoon salt
½ cup finely chopped sweetened, flaked coconut*
¼ cup finely chopped toasted pecans
1 recipe Italian Cream Cheese Frosting (recipe follows)
Garnish: chopped, toasted pecans

- Preheat oven to 350°.
- Line 17 wells of 2 (12-well) muffin pans with paper liners.
- In a large mixing bowl, beat butter at medium speed with an electric mixer until creamy. Gradually add sugar, beating until light and fluffy, approximately 3 minutes. Add eggs, one at a time, beating well after each addition.
- In a small bowl, combine sour cream and milk, stirring to blend. Add vanilla extract.
- In a medium bowl, combine flour, baking powder, and salt, whisking well. Add flour mixture to butter mixture in thirds, alternately with sour cream mixture, beginning and ending with flour mixture. Reduce mixer speed to low, and add coconut and pecans, beating until just combined.
- Using a levered 3-tablespoon scoop, divide batter among prepared wells of muffin pans.
- Bake until cupcakes are golden brown and a wooden pick inserted in the centers comes out clean, 16 to 18 minutes. Let cool slightly in pans. When cupcakes are cool enough to handle, transfer to a wire rack, and let cool completely.
- Place Italian Cream Cheese Frosting in a piping bag fitted with a large open-star tip (Wilton #1). Pipe frosting onto cooled cupcakes in a decorative swirl.
- Garnish with pecans, if desired.
- Refrigerate cupcakes, covered, until serving time.

*An easy way to finely chop coconut is to pulse it in the work bowl of a food processor. Pulse first, then measure coconut.

Italian Cream Cheese Frosting
Yield: 3 cups

½ cup salted butter, softened
1 (8-ounce) package cream cheese, softened
4¼ cups confectioners' sugar
1 teaspoon vanilla extract
⅛ teaspoon salt

• In a large mixing bowl, combine butter and cream cheese. Beat at high speed with an electric mixer until creamy. Add confectioners' sugar, vanilla extract, and salt. Beginning at low speed and gradually increasing to high speed, beat until frosting is light and fluffy.

Make-Ahead Tip: Frosting can be made a day in advance and refrigerated in a covered container until needed. Before using, beat at high speed with an electric mixer until softened and spreadable, approximately 1 minute.

Earl Grey–Chocolate Cakes
Yield: 24

½ cup water
3 (.2-ounce) bags Earl Grey black tea
2½ cups sifted cake flour
1½ cups sugar
¾ cup unsweetened dark cocoa powder
2 teaspoons baking soda
1 teaspoon salt
½ cup plus 2 tablespoons salted butter, softened
2 large eggs
2 teaspoons vanilla extract
1 cup whole buttermilk
1 recipe Dark Chocolate Ganache (recipe follows)
Garnish: Wilton Cookies & Crème Crunch Sprinkles and dark chocolate shards

• Preheat oven to 350°.
• Spray a 13x9-inch baking pan with nonstick cooking spray.
• In a small saucepan, heat water to boiling. Remove from heat, and add tea bags. Cover, and let steep for 5 minutes. Remove and discard tea bags. Let tea cool to room temperature.
• In a large mixing bowl, combine flour, sugar, cocoa powder, baking soda, and salt, whisking well. Add butter, eggs, vanilla extract, buttermilk, and tea. Beat at medium speed with an electric mixer for 3 minutes.
• Pour batter into prepared baking pan, and spread evenly.
• Bake until a wooden pick inserted in the center comes out clean, 28 to 30 minutes. Let cool in pan on a wire rack for 10 minutes. Invert onto a wire rack, and let cool completely.

Earl Grey-Chocolate Cakes

• Using a long, serrated knife, trim top of cake to create a level surface, if necessary. Cut cake into 24 (2-inch) squares.
• Place cake squares on a wire rack, and spoon warm Dark Chocolate Ganache over each square, letting ganache drip down sides. Smooth ganache with an offset spatula to cover cake squares, if necessary.
• Garnish with sprinkles and dark chocolate shards, if desired.

Dark Chocolate Ganache
Yield: 3 cups

2 cups heavy whipping cream
6 (.2-ounce) bags Earl Grey black tea
1 (10-ounce) package bittersweet chocolate morsels

• In a small saucepan, heat cream until hot but not boiling. Remove from heat, and add tea bags. Cover, and let steep for 15 minutes. Remove and discard tea bags. Reheat cream until hot but not boiling. Remove from heat, and add chocolate morsels, stirring until chocolate is melted and smooth. Use immediately.

Triple-Layer Pumpkin Cakes

Triple-Layer Pumpkin Cakes
Yield: 12

- ½ cup salted butter, softened
- 1¼ cups firmly packed light brown sugar
- 2 large eggs
- 1 cup canned pumpkin purée
- 1½ teaspoons vanilla extract
- 2 cups sifted cake flour
- 1 teaspoon ground cinnamon
- ½ teaspoon baking powder
- ½ teaspoon baking soda
- ½ teaspoon salt
- ½ teaspoon ground ginger
- ¼ teaspoon ground nutmeg
- ½ cup whole buttermilk
- 1 recipe Orange–Cream Cheese Frosting (recipe follows)

- Preheat oven to 350°.
- Spray an 18x13-inch rimmed baking sheet with nonstick cooking spray. Line with parchment paper, and spray again.
- In a large mixing bowl, beat butter at medium-high speed with an electric mixer until creamy. Add brown sugar, and beat until light and fluffy, approximately 3 minutes. Add eggs, one at a time, beating well after each addition. Add pumpkin purée and vanilla extract, beating until incorporated.
- In a medium bowl, combine flour, cinnamon, baking powder, baking soda, salt, ginger, and nutmeg, whisking well. Add flour mixture to butter mixture in thirds, alternately with buttermilk, beginning and ending with flour mixture. Spread batter into prepared pan, rapping sharply on countertop to reduce air bubbles.
- Bake until a wooden pick inserted in the center comes out clean, 13 to 14 minutes. Let cool completely in pan on a wire rack.
- Remove cake from pan, and place on a cutting board. Cut cake into 3 (13x6-inch) portions. Using an offset spatula, spread one-fourth of Orange–Cream Cheese Frosting on 1 portion of cake. Top with another portion of cake, and spread one-third of remaining frosting on top. Top with remaining portion of cake, and spread with half of remaining frosting. Freeze assembled cake until it is firm enough to cut into cake fingers, approximately 1 hour.
- Trim rough edges from all sides of cake. Using a long, sharp knife, cut cake evenly into 12 pieces, pressing downward with knife to create a clean cut. Place cake pieces on a serving platter.
- Place remaining frosting in a pastry bag fitted with a closed-star tip (Ateco #30). Pipe frosting shells in rows on tops of cake pieces.
- Let come to room temperature before serving.

Make-Ahead Tip: Cake can be baked, frosted, and assembled a week in advance. Wrap securely in plastic wrap, and freeze until needed. Cut cake into fingers while frozen. Let thaw before piping frosting shells on top.

Kitchen Tip: To create even layers of frosting, measure equal amounts to spread between layers.

Orange–Cream Cheese Frosting
Yield: 5 cups

- 11 ounces cream cheese, softened
- ¾ cup salted butter, softened
- 7 cups confectioners' sugar
- 2 teaspoons vanilla extract
- 1 tablespoon fresh orange zest

- In a large mixing bowl, beat cream cheese and butter at high speed with an electric mixer until smooth and creamy. Add confectioners' sugar and vanilla extract, beating until incorporated. Beat frosting at high speed until light and fluffy. Add orange zest, beating to combine.

Make-Ahead Tip: Orange–Cream Cheese Frosting can be made a day in advance and refrigerated, covered, until needed.

> "All true tea lovers not only like their tea strong, but like it a little stronger with each year that passes."
>
> —George Orwell

Chocolate-Chai Cake Bites

Chocolate-Chai Cake Bites
Gluten-free | Yield: 15

½ cup sugar
¼ cup natural unsweetened cocoa powder
1 tablespoon finely ground white cornmeal
1 teaspoon ground ginger
½ teaspoon ground Vietnamese cinnamon
½ teaspoon ground cardamom
¼ teaspoon ground cloves
⅛ teaspoon salt
2 large eggs, lightly beaten
¼ cup salted butter, melted
1¼ teaspoons vanilla extract
1 recipe Sweetened Whipped Cream (see recipe on page 185)
Garnish: grated chocolate

- Preheat oven to 325°.
- Spray 15 wells of a 24-well, shallow mini muffin pan* with nonstick cooking spray.
- In a large bowl, combine sugar, cocoa powder, cornmeal, ginger, cinnamon, cardamom, cloves, and salt, whisking well.
- In a medium bowl, combine eggs, melted butter, and vanilla extract, whisking well. Add to cocoa mixture, whisking until incorporated. Fill prepared wells of pan approximately three-quarters full (approximately 1 tablespoon batter per well).
- Bake until puffed, 11 to 12 minutes. (Surface will look slightly dry but will still be moist in center.) Let cool in pan for 5 minutes. Carefully transfer to a wire rack, and let cool completely.
- Place Sweetened Whipped Cream in a piping bag fitted with an open-star tip (Ateco #848). Pipe cream onto cooled cake bites.
- Garnish with grated chocolate, if desired.
- Serve immediately.

*We used a Chicago Metallic mini muffin pan with shallow wells (approximately ¾ inch in depth), which is available at chicagometallicbakeware.com.

Strawberry-Ginger Roulade
Yield: approximately 14 servings

3 tablespoons fresh orange juice
1 cup plus 3 tablespoons sugar, divided
3 cups thinly sliced strawberries
4 large eggs, separated
1½ teaspoons vanilla extract, divided
¾ cup sifted cake flour
¾ teaspoon baking powder
½ teaspoon salt
¼ cup finely chopped crystallized ginger
Confectioners' sugar
2 cups heavy whipping cream
Garnish: additional confectioners' sugar and fresh strawberries

- Preheat oven to 375°.
- Spray 2 (9-inch) square cake pans with nonstick cooking spray. Line pans with parchment paper. Spray again.
- In a medium bowl, combine orange juice and 3 tablespoons sugar, stirring until sugar dissolves. Add strawberries, tossing to coat. Let stand at room temperature for 1 hour.
- Meanwhile, in a mixing bowl, beat egg yolks at medium speed with an electric mixer until light in color, 2 to 3 minutes. Add ¾ cup sugar and 1 teaspoon vanilla extract, beating until incorporated, 1 to 2 minutes.
- In a medium bowl, combine flour, baking powder, and salt, whisking well. Gradually add flour mixture to egg mixture, beating until smooth.
- In a separate bowl, beat egg whites at high speed with an electric mixer until stiff peaks form. Gently fold egg whites and ginger into batter. Divide batter evenly between prepared pans.
- Bake until layers are light golden brown and a wooden pick inserted in the centers comes out clean, approximately 6 minutes.
- While cakes are baking, sift confectioners' sugar over 2 clean thin dish towels in 9-inch squares.
- When cakes are done, immediately turn out onto prepared dish towels. Remove parchment paper, and roll up each cake jelly-roll style in dish towel, setting each one seam side down on wire racks to cool.
- In a large mixing bowl, combine cream, remaining ¼ cup sugar, and remaining ½ teaspoon vanilla extract. Beat at medium-high speed with an electric mixer until stiff peaks form. Add enough liquid from strawberry mixture to tint cream pink, stirring gently.
- Gently unroll cakes, and spread each with half of whipped-cream mixture. Place half of sliced strawberries in a single layer over each whipped-cream layer. Reroll cakes jelly-roll style, placing seam side down. Cover, and refrigerate for up to 1 day until ready to serve.
- Just before serving, garnish each roulade with a dusting of confectioners' sugar, if desired. Using a serrated knife, trim ends of roulades to even. Slice roulades into 1-inch pieces.
- Garnish with fresh strawberries, if desired.

Strawberry-Ginger Roulade

Tarts and Cheesecakes

LEMON, WHITE CHOCOLATE & MASCARPONE FLOWER TARTLETS
(recipe on page 190)

Strawberry-Mascarpone Tartlets

Strawberry-Mascarpone Tartlets
Yield: 8

1 (8-ounce) container mascarpone cheese, softened
½ cup strawberry preserves
¼ teaspoon vanilla extract
1 pinch salt
1 (14.1-ounce) package refrigerated pie dough (2 sheets)
4 cups whole strawberries
Garnish: melted strawberry jelly

• In a small bowl, combine mascarpone cheese, strawberry preserves, vanilla extract, and salt, stirring to blend. Cover and refrigerate for 2 hours.
• Preheat oven to 450°.
• On a lightly floured surface, unroll both sheets of pie dough. Using a 4-inch round cutter, cut circles from pie dough. Press into 8 (4-inch) round tartlet pans with removable bottoms, as illustrated on page 232. Using a fork, prick bottoms of dough. Place prepared tartlet pans on 2 rimmed baking sheets. Refrigerate for 30 minutes.
• Bake until light golden brown, 6 to 7 minutes. Let cool completely on baking sheets.
• Divide mascarpone mixture evenly among cooled tartlet shells, smoothing to create a level surface.
• Reserve 4 strawberries for tops of tartlets. Hull remaining strawberries and cut in half. Place 1 strawberry half in center of each tartlet. Arrange remaining strawberry halves in a circle with tips pointing toward center of tartlets and propping on center strawberry. Cut reserved strawberries in half. Top each tartlet with a strawberry half.
• Garnish strawberries with a light coating of melted jelly, if desired.

Make-Ahead Tip: Tartlet shells and filling can be made earlier in the day. Assemble tartlets up to 2 hours before serving. Refrigerate, covered, until serving time.

Chocolate Chess Tartlets
Yield: 16

1 (14.1-ounce) package refrigerated pie dough (2 sheets)
2 large eggs, lightly beaten
½ cup semisweet chocolate morsels, melted
⅓ cup sugar
4 tablespoons salted butter, melted
1 tablespoon finely ground white cornmeal
1¼ teaspoons vanilla extract
⅛ teaspoon salt
1 recipe Sweetened Whipped Cream (recipe follows)
Garnish: mini chocolate curls

- Preheat oven to 450°.
- Lightly spray 16 (2½-inch) round tartlet pans with nonstick cooking spray. Place on a rimmed baking sheet.
- On a lightly floured surface, unroll both sheets of pie dough. Using a 3-inch round cutter, cut 16 circles from dough. Press dough circles into prepared tartlet pans, as illustrated on page 232. Using a fork, prick bottoms of dough. Refrigerate for 30 minutes.
- Bake until light golden brown, 5 to 6 minutes. Let tartlet shells cool completely on baking sheet.
- In a medium bowl, combine eggs, melted chocolate, sugar, melted butter, cornmeal, vanilla extract, and salt, whisking to blend. Divide chocolate mixture among cooled tartlet shells, filling each three-quarters full.
- Bake until mixture is set and slightly puffed, 8 to 10 minutes. Let tartlets cool completely before removing from tartlet pans. (As tartlets cool, slight cracks will form in surface.)
- Place Sweetened Whipped Cream in a piping bag fitted with a large open-star tip (Wilton #1). Pipe a whipped cream rosette onto each tartlet.
- Garnish with chocolate curls, if desired.

Kitchen Tip: *To make mini chocolate curls, grate a chocolate bar, using a citrus zester.*

Sweetened Whipped Cream
Yield: 1 cup

½ cup cold heavy whipping cream
1 tablespoon confectioners' sugar
¼ teaspoon vanilla extract

- In a small bowl, combine cream, confectioners' sugar, and vanilla extract. Beat at high speed with an electric mixer until thickened and creamy.
- Refrigerate in an airtight container until needed.

Chocolate Chess Tartlets

PEACH FLOWER
how-to on page 234

Peach-Ginger Tartlets

Peach-Ginger Tartlets
Yield: 6

- 40 vanilla-wafer cookies
- 3 tablespoons sugar
- 5 tablespoons salted butter, melted
- 1 (8-ounce) package cream cheese, softened
- 3 tablespoons honey
- 1 tablespoon heavy whipping cream
- 1 teaspoon ground ginger
- 1 (29-ounce) can peach halves in heavy syrup

- Preheat oven to 350°.
- In the work bowl of a food processor, process cookies until finely ground.
- In a medium bowl, combine cookie crumbs, sugar, and melted butter, stirring to blend. Divide evenly among 6 (4-inch) tartlet pans with removable bottoms, pressing crumb mixture firmly into bottom and up sides of pans.
- Bake until golden brown, approximately 8 minutes. Let cool completely. Freeze to harden shells, approximately 2 hours. (This will prevent breakage when assembling tartlets.)
- In a medium mixing bowl, combine cream cheese, honey, cream, and ginger. Beat at high speed with an electric mixer until smooth and creamy.
- Reserving syrup, lay peach halves on a cutting board, rounded side up. Using a paring knife, cut peach halves into thin vertical slices, approximately ¼ inch thick.
- Remove tartlet shells from pans. Divide cream cheese mixture among frozen tartlet shells, spreading in an even layer.
- Beginning with longest slices, build a flower shape with peaches, overlapping ends of slices.
- Brush tartlets with reserved syrup. Serve immediately, or refrigerate, lightly covered, for up to an hour before serving.

Lemon-Chamomile Tartlets
Yield: 48

- 2 boxes mini (1.75-inch) shortbread tartlet shells
- 6 tablespoons heavy whipping cream
- 3 bags chamomile-citrus tea
- 2 large eggs
- ½ cup sugar
- 2 teaspoons fresh lemon zest
- ¼ cup fresh lemon juice
- 1 recipe Meringue Topping (recipe follows)

- Preheat oven to 325°.
- Place tartlet shells on 2 rimmed baking sheets.
- Heat cream to very hot but not boiling. Remove from heat, add tea bags, and let steep for 15 minutes. Discard tea bags. Let cool.

Lemon-Chamomile Tartlets

- In a medium bowl, combine eggs, sugar, lemon zest, lemon juice, and cooled cream, whisking to blend. Transfer mixture to a large measuring cup with a pouring spout for ease of filling tartlet shells. (Keep mixture whisked so that it does not settle.) Fill tartlet shells to just below rim.
- Bake until filling is set, approximately 10 minutes. Remove tartlets from oven.
- Increase oven temperature to 350°.
- Place Meringue Topping in a piping bag fitted with a large open-star tip (Wilton #1). Pipe a decorative swirl on top of warm tartlets.
- Return tartlets to oven, and bake until Meringue Topping is golden brown, 5 to 7 minutes.
- Serve immediately, or refrigerate until needed.

Meringue Topping
Yield: 2 cups

- 2 egg whites, at room temperature
- 3 tablespoons sugar
- ¼ teaspoon cream of tartar

- In a mixing bowl, combine egg whites, sugar, and cream of tartar. Beat at high speed with an electric mixer until stiff peaks form. Use immediately.

Key Lime Mini Cheesecakes

Key Lime Mini Cheesecakes
Yield: 12

¾ cup graham cracker crumbs
⅓ cup plus 1 tablespoon sugar, divided
3 tablespoons salted butter, melted
1 (8-ounce) package cream cheese, softened
2 tablespoons bottled Key lime juice
3 teaspoons all-purpose flour
1 teaspoon fresh lime zest
1 large egg
Garnish: fresh lime slices

• Preheat oven to 350°.
• Lightly spray a 12-well mini cheesecake pan with nonstick cooking spray.
• In a small bowl, combine graham cracker crumbs, 1 tablespoon sugar, and melted butter, stirring to blend. Divide crumb mixture evenly among wells of prepared pan, pressing firmly to create a level base.
• Bake until golden brown, approximately 6 minutes. Let cool completely.
• In a medium mixing bowl, combine cream cheese, remaining ⅓ cup sugar, lime juice, flour, and lime zest. Beat at high speed with an electric mixer until smooth and creamy. With mixer running at medium speed, add egg, beating until incorporated. Divide mixture evenly among wells of prepared pan.
• Bake until filling is set and slightly puffed, approximately 11 minutes. Let cool completely. (Cheesecakes will fall as they cool.) Refrigerate for at least 4 hours.
• Remove cheesecakes from pan.
• Garnish each with a lime slice before serving, if desired.

Make-Ahead Tip: *Cheesecakes can be made a day in advance and refrigerated (ungarnished) in an airtight container. Garnish before serving. Or freeze (ungarnished) in an airtight container for up to a week. Let thaw completely before garnishing.*

Peppermint Mini Cheesecakes
Yield: 12

¾ cup graham cracker crumbs
¼ cup plus 1 tablespoon sugar, divided
3 tablespoons salted butter, melted
1 (8-ounce) package cream cheese, softened
3 teaspoons all-purpose flour
½ teaspoon vanilla extract
1 large egg
¼ cup peppermint baking chips*
1 recipe Sweetened Whipped Cream (recipe on page 185)
Garnish: peppermint candy

• Preheat oven to 350°.
• Lightly spray a 12-well mini cheesecake pan with nonstick cooking spray.
• In a small bowl, combine graham cracker crumbs, 1 tablespoon sugar, and melted butter, stirring to blend. Divide crumb mixture evenly among wells of prepared pan, pressing to create a level base.
• Bake until golden brown, approximately 6 minutes. Let cool completely.
• In a medium bowl, combine cream cheese, remaining ¼ cup sugar, flour, and vanilla extract. Beat at high speed with an electric mixer until smooth and creamy. With mixer running at medium speed, add egg, beating until incorporated. Add peppermint baking chips, stirring to combine. Divide mixture evenly among wells of prepared pan.
• Bake until filling is set and slightly puffed, 10 to 11 minutes. Let cool completely. (Cheesecakes will fall as they cool.) Refrigerate, covered, for at least 4 hours.
• Remove cheesecakes from pan.
• Place Sweetened Whipped Cream in a piping bag fitted with a large open-star tip (Wilton #1). Pipe a whipped-cream rosette onto each cheesecake.
• Garnish each with peppermint candies, if desired.

*We used Andes Peppermint Crunch Baking Chips.

Peppermint Mini Cheesecakes

Pineapple, Coconut & Macadamia Custard Tartlets

Pineapple, Coconut & Macadamia Custard Tartlets
Yield: 6

1 (14.1-ounce) package refrigerated pie dough (2 sheets)
1 (8-ounce) can crushed pineapple, undrained
½ cup plus 2 tablespoons sugar, divided
2 large eggs, separated
1 tablespoon cornstarch
1 tablespoon fresh lemon juice
⅛ teaspoon salt
1 tablespoon salted butter
¼ cup toasted sweetened flaked coconut
¼ cup chopped macadamia nuts
¼ teaspoon cream of tartar

- Preheat oven to 450°.
- On a lightly floured surface, unroll both sheets of pie dough on a lightly floured surface. Using a 4½-inch round cutter, cut 6 circles from pie dough. Press dough circles into 6 (4-inch) round tartlet pans with removable bottoms, as illustrated on page 232. Using a fork, prick bottoms of dough. Place prepared tartlet pans on a rimmed baking sheet. Refrigerate for 30 minutes.
- Bake until light golden brown, 6 to 7 minutes. Let cool completely on baking sheet.
- In a medium nonstick sauté pan, combine pineapple, ½ cup sugar, egg yolks, cornstarch, lemon juice, and salt, stirring to blend. Cook over medium heat, stirring until thickened. Add butter, stirring until melted and incorporated. Remove from heat, and let cool slightly. Add coconut and macadamia nuts. Spoon mixture into cooled tartlet shells.
- Reduce oven temperature to 375°.
- In a medium bowl, combine egg whites, remaining 2 tablespoons sugar, and cream of tartar. Beat at high speed with an electric mixer until stiff peaks form. Divide meringue evenly among tartlets, swirling with a spoon to create peaks.
- Bake until peaks of meringue are golden brown, approximately 8 minutes. Let cool slightly, and remove tartlets from tartlet pans.
- Serve at room temperature, or refrigerate, covered, for 4 hours and serve cold.

Make-Ahead Tip: *Tartlets can be made earlier in the day and refrigerated, lightly covered, until serving time.*

Lemon, White Chocolate & Mascarpone Flower Tartlets
Yield: 16

1 cup salted butter, softened
1 cup sugar
1 large egg
1 tablespoon whole milk
1 teaspoon vanilla extract
3 cups all-purpose flour
¾ teaspoon baking powder
¼ teaspoon salt
Confectioners' sugar
1 recipe Lemon–White Chocolate Mousse (recipe follows)
Garnish: fresh raspberries and fresh mint

- In a large bowl, combine butter and sugar. Beat at medium speed with an electric mixer until creamy. Add egg, milk, and vanilla extract, beating to combine.
- In a medium bowl, combine flour, baking powder, and salt. Gradually add flour mixture to butter mixture, beating well to combine. Divide dough in half, and wrap each half tightly in plastic wrap. Refrigerate for 2 hours.
- Preheat oven to 375°.
- Spray 2 (12-well) whoopee pie pans with nonstick baking spray with flour.
- On a lightly floured surface, roll each portion of dough to a ¼-inch thickness. Using a 3½-inch flower-shaped cutter dipped in flour, cut

Lemon, White Chocolate & Mascarpone Flower Tartlets

out 16 shapes from dough. Place in wells of prepared pan. Using a fork, prick bottoms of dough.
• Bake until edges are lightly browned, approximately 7 minutes. Let cool in pans for 10 minutes. Remove tartlet shells from pan, and let cool completely on wire racks.
• Lightly sift confectioners' sugar over tops and bottoms of tartlet shells.
• Place Lemon–White Chocolate Mousse in a piping bag fitted with a large open-star tip (Wilton #1). Pipe mousse rosettes into each tartlet shell.
• Garnish with raspberries and mint, if desired.
• Serve immediately.

Lemon–White Chocolate Mousse
Yield: 4 cups

2 (10-ounce) jars lemon curd
2 (8-ounce) containers mascarpone cheese
2 (4-ounce) bars white chocolate, melted

• In a large bowl, whisk lemon curd vigorously to loosen. Add mascarpone cheese, whisking until incorporated. Add melted white chocolate, whisking to blend.
• Refrigerate in a covered container for at least 1 hour until needed.

Sweet Potato Tartlets

Sweet Potato Tartlets

Yield: 6

3 cups cubed raw sweet potatoes
1 (14.1-ounce) package refrigerated pie dough (2 sheets)
2 tablespoons salted butter, melted
¼ cup sugar
2 tablespoons heavy whipping cream
2 tablespoons whole milk
¾ teaspoon vanilla extract
¼ teaspoon ground cinnamon
⅛ teaspoon ground nutmeg
⅛ teaspoon salt
1 large egg
1 recipe Sweetened Whipped Cream (recipe on page 185)
Garnish: ground nutmeg

- Preheat oven to 350°.
- Place sweet potatoes in a medium saucepan with enough water to cover. Bring to a boil over medium heat. Cover, and cook until tender, approximately 15 minutes. Drain sweet potatoes, and let cool. Using a potato masher, mash sweet potatoes. (You should have approximately 1½ cups.)
- On a lightly floured surface, unroll both sheets of pie dough. Using a 4½-inch round cutter, cut 6 circles from pie dough. Press into 6 (4-inch) tartlet pans with removable bottoms, as illustrated on page 232. Place prepared pans on a rimmed baking sheet.
- In a large mixing bowl, combine sweet potatoes, melted butter, sugar, cream, milk, vanilla extract, cinnamon, nutmeg, and salt. Beat at medium speed with an electric mixer until smooth. Add egg, beating well. Divide mixture evenly among prepared tartlet shells.
- Bake until filling is set and a knife inserted in the centers comes out clean, 30 to 35 minutes. Let cool completely before removing tartlets from pans.
- Place Sweetened Whipped Cream in a piping bag fitted with a small closed-star tip (Ateco #30). Pipe rosettes onto surfaces of tartlets.
- Garnish each with a dusting of ground nutmeg, if desired.
- Serve at room temperature, or refrigerate, covered, until needed, and serve cold.

Chocolate–Peanut Butter Tartlets

Yield: 24

½ cup peanut butter morsels
1 cup plus 2 tablespoons heavy whipping cream, divided
2 tablespoons creamy peanut butter
1 (4-ounce) bar bittersweet chocolate, finely chopped
1 box mini (1.75-inch) shortbread tartlet shells
2 tablespoons confectioners' sugar
½ teaspoon vanilla extract
Garnish: mini dark chocolate curls

Chocolate–Peanut Butter Tartlets

- In a medium microwave-safe bowl, combine peanut butter morsels and 2 tablespoons cream. Microwave at 50 percent power for 15-second intervals until melted, approximately 1½ minutes. Stir until smooth. Add peanut butter, stirring until combined. Let cool slightly.
- In a small saucepan, heat ½ cup cream almost to boiling. Remove from heat, and add chocolate. Let mixture stand for 1 minute. Stir until smooth.
- Place tartlet shells on a small tray. Divide chocolate mixture evenly among tartlet shells. Refrigerate until chocolate is firm, approximately 30 minutes.
- In a small bowl, combine remaining ½ cup cream, confectioners' sugar, and vanilla extract. Beat at medium speed with an electric mixer until thick, stopping just before stiff peaks form. Add cream mixture to cooled peanut butter mixture, whisking well.
- Transfer mixture to a piping bag fitted with a large open-star tip (Wilton #1). Pipe onto tartlets.
- Garnish with chocolate curls, if desired.

Kitchen Tip: To make mini chocolate curls, grate a chocolate bar, using a citrus zester.

Make-Ahead Tip: Tartlets can be made earlier in the day and refrigerated (without peanut butter whipped cream) in an airtight container. Let come to room temperature before garnishing and serving.

Brownie Tart

Brownie Tart

Yield: 8 to 10 servings

½ cup salted butter
4 tablespoons natural unsweetened cocoa powder
1 cup sugar
½ cup all-purpose flour
1 teaspoon baking powder
¼ teaspoon salt
2 large eggs
1 teaspoon vanilla extract
1 cup chopped, toasted pecans
Garnish: confectioners' sugar and strawberries

- Preheat oven to 350°.
- Spray a 9-inch round tart pan with a removable bottom with nonstick baking spray with flour. Sprinkle additional flour along the seam of removable bottom to prevent batter from leaking. Set aside.
- In a medium saucepan, melt butter over low heat. Add cocoa powder, stirring until smooth and creamy. Remove pan from heat, and set aside.
- In a medium bowl, combine sugar, flour, baking powder, and salt, whisking well. Add eggs and vanilla extract to butter mixture. Add flour mixture, stirring until ingredients are thoroughly blended. Add pecans, stirring to combine. Spread batter evenly in prepared tart pan.
- Bake until a wooden pick inserted in the center comes out with only a few crumbs clinging to it, approximately 23 minutes. Let tart cool completely before removing from pan.
- Garnish by sifting confectioners' sugar over top of tart and arranging strawberries in the center, if desired.

Kitchen Tip: *Tart can be made in a 9-inch pie pan, and pieces cut and served from pan.*

Make-Ahead Tip: *Tart can be made in advance, cooled completely, wrapped securely in plastic wrap, placed in an airtight container, and frozen for up to a week. Let thaw completely before garnishing.*

Pistachio-Orange Tartlets

Yield: 12

1 (14.1-ounce) package refrigerated pie dough (2 sheets)
1 large egg
½ cup firmly packed light brown sugar
3 tablespoons light corn syrup
1 tablespoon salted butter, melted
1 teaspoon vanilla extract
1 teaspoon fresh orange zest
½ cup plus 2 tablespoons finely chopped roasted, salted pistachios
Garnish: fresh orange zest curls

Pistachio-Orange Tartlets

- Preheat oven to 450°.
- Lightly spray 12 (4x2¼-inch) diamond-shaped tartlet pans with nonstick cooking spray.
- On a lightly floured surface, unroll both sheets of pie dough. Using a tartlet pan as a guide, cut 12 shapes from pie dough. Press dough shapes into prepared tartlet pans, as illustrated on page 232. Using a fork, prick bottoms of dough. Place prepared tartlet pans on a rimmed baking sheet. Refrigerate for 30 minutes.
- Bake until very light golden brown, 5 to 7 minutes. Let cool completely on baking sheet.
- Reduce oven temperature to 350°.
- In a medium bowl, combine egg, brown sugar, corn syrup, melted butter, vanilla extract, and orange zest, whisking to blend. Add pistachios, stirring to combine. Divide mixture evenly among cooled tartlet shells, filling each three-quarters full.
- Bake until filling is set and slightly puffed, approximately 13 minutes. Let cool completely in pans. Remove tartlets from pans.
- Garnish each with an orange zest curl, if desired.

Kitchen tip: *Pistachios in the shell tend to be a brighter green than shelled pistachios. To give these tartlets their best color, we recommend buying pistachios in the shell and shelling your own.*

Blueberry-Lemon Mini Cheesecakes

Blueberry-Lemon Mini Cheesecakes
Yield: 12

¾ cup graham cracker crumbs
⅓ cup plus 1 tablespoon sugar, divided
3 tablespoons salted butter, melted
1 (8-ounce) package cream cheese, softened
3 teaspoons all-purpose flour
1 teaspoon fresh lemon zest
2 tablespoons fresh lemon juice
1 large egg
Garnish: fresh blueberries and fresh mint

- Preheat oven to 350°.
- Lightly spray a 12-well mini cheesecake pan with nonstick cooking spray.
- In a small bowl, combine graham cracker crumbs, 1 tablespoon sugar, and melted butter, stirring to blend. Divide crumb mixture evenly among wells of prepared pan, pressing firmly to create a level base.
- Bake until golden brown, approximately 6 minutes. Let cool completely.
- In a medium bowl, combine cream cheese, remaining ⅓ cup sugar, flour, lemon zest, and lemon juice. Beat at medium speed with an electric mixer until smooth and creamy. With mixer running at medium speed, add egg, beating until incorporated. Divide mixture evenly among wells of prepared pan.
- Bake until filling is set and slightly puffed, approximately 11 minutes. Let cool completely. (Cheesecakes will fall as they cool.) Refrigerate, covered, for at least 4 hours.
- Remove cheesecakes from pan.
- Garnish with blueberries* and mint before serving, if desired.

*For additional sweetness, toss blueberries in simple syrup, if desired.

Make-Ahead Tip: *Cheesecakes can be made a day in advance and refrigerated (ungarnished) in an airtight container. Garnish before serving. Or freeze (ungarnished) in an airtight container for up to 1 week. Let thaw completely before garnishing.*

Decadent Chocolate Mini Cheesecakes
Yield: 12

¾ cup chocolate wafer crumbs
¼ cup plus 1 tablespoon sugar, divided
3 tablespoons salted butter, melted
1 (8-ounce) package cream cheese, softened
3 teaspoons all-purpose flour
½ teaspoon vanilla extract
1 egg
1 (4-ounce) bittersweet chocolate bar, melted
1 recipe Semisweet Ganache (recipe follows)
Garnish: fresh raspberries and fresh mint

Decadent Chocolate Mini Cheesecakes

- Preheat oven to 350°.
- Lightly spray a 12-well, square mini cheesecake pan with nonstick cooking spray.
- In a small bowl, combine chocolate wafer crumbs, 1 tablespoon sugar, and melted butter, stirring to blend. Divide crumb mixture evenly among wells of prepared pan, pressing firmly to create a level base.
- Bake until set, approximately 6 minutes. Let cool completely.
- In a medium bowl, combine cream cheese, remaining ¼ cup sugar, flour, and vanilla extract. Beat at high speed with an electric mixer until smooth and creamy. With mixer running on medium speed, add egg, beating until incorporated. Add melted chocolate, beating until incorporated. Divide mixture evenly among wells of prepared pan.
- Bake until cheesecakes are set and slightly puffed, 10 to 11 minutes. Let cool completely. Refrigerate, covered, for at least 4 hours.
- Remove cheesecakes from pan just before serving. Spread Semisweet Ganache onto cheesecakes.
- Garnish with raspberries and mint, if desired.

Make-Ahead Tip: *Cheesecakes can be made a day in advance and refrigerated (ungarnished, without raspberries and mint) in an airtight container. Garnish before serving. Or freeze (ungarnished) in an airtight container for up to a week. Let thaw completely before garnishing.*

Semisweet Ganache
Yield: ⅓ cup

¼ cup heavy whipping cream
½ cup semisweet chocolate morsels

- In a small saucepan, heat cream over medium-high heat until very hot with bubbles forming around edges of pan. Remove from heat, and add chocolate morsels. Stir until chocolate is melted and mixture is smooth and creamy.

Cookies AND Bars

STENCILED GINGERBREAD COOKIES
(recipe on page 215)

Lemon-Lime Spritz Cookies
Yield: 46

1 cup salted butter, softened
½ cup plus 2 tablespoons sugar
1 large egg
1 teaspoon vanilla extract
1 teaspoon lemon extract
1 teaspoon lime zest
2¼ cups all-purpose flour
¾ cup prepared lemon curd
Garnish: additional lime zest

- Preheat oven to 350°.
- Line several rimmed baking sheets with parchment paper.
- In a large mixing bowl, combine butter and sugar. Beat with a mixer at medium-high speed until light and creamy, 2 to 3 minutes. Add egg, vanilla extract, lemon extract, and lime zest, beating until blended. Add flour, beating until combined.
- Transfer dough to a piping bag fitted with very large open-star tip (Ateco #848). Pipe rosettes of dough onto prepared baking sheets. Using the back of a round ½-teaspoon measuring spoon, make an indentation in the center of each cookie.
- Bake until cookies are set and edges are very light brown, approximately 12 minutes. Transfer to wire racks, and let cool completely.
- Just before serving, place lemon curd in a piping bag fitted with a medium round tip (Wilton #12), and pipe a button of lemon curd into center of each cookie.
- Garnish with additional lime zest, if desired.

Make-Ahead Tip: *Cookies can be baked and then frozen in an airtight container up to one week in advance. Let thaw completely before filling and garnishing.*

Lemon-Lime Spritz Cookies

Blueberry Crumb Bars
Yield: 12

1½ cups quick-cooking oats
¾ cup firmly packed light brown sugar
½ teaspoon ground cinnamon
¾ cup cold salted butter, cut into pieces
½ cup sugar
3 tablespoons cornstarch
¼ teaspoon salt
4 cups fresh blueberries
½ cup orange juice
1 tablespoon fresh lemon juice
½ teaspoon vanilla extract

- Preheat oven to 350°.
- Line an 8-inch square pan with heavy-duty foil, letting foil hang over sides of pan to create handles. Line foil with parchment paper. Spray with cooking spray.
- In a medium bowl, combine oats, brown sugar, and cinnamon, whisking well. Using a pastry blender, cut butter into oats mixture until incorporated. Continue to work mixture with hands, rubbing butter into oats mixture until very moist and crumbly. Reserve 1 cup crumb mixture for topping.
- Press remaining crumb mixture into bottom of prepared pan, smoothing to create a level surface.
- In a medium saucepan, combine sugar, cornstarch, and salt, whisking to blend. Add blueberries, orange juice, and lemon juice, stirring to blend. Cook over medium heat, stirring constantly, until mixture comes to a boil and thickens. Reduce heat to low, and cook 3 to 4 minutes more, stirring frequently. Remove from heat, and add vanilla extract. Let cool completely.
- Spread cooled blueberry mixture over prepared crust. Sprinkle evenly with reserved crumb mixture.
- Bake until filling is set and topping is golden brown, 40 to 45 minutes. Let cool completely.
- Using foil handles, lift from pan, and place on a cutting surface. Cut into bars, trimming and discarding edges.
- Store in a covered container at room temperature.

Make-Ahead Tip: Blueberry Crumb Bars can be made a week in advance and frozen whole in an airtight container. Cut into bars while frozen. Let thaw before serving.

Kitchen Tip: Bars are easier to cut when refrigerated until very cold, approximately 4 hours.

Blueberry Crumb Bars

Chocolate-Dipped Peanut Butter Cookies

Chocolate-Dipped Peanut Butter Cookies
Gluten-free | *Yield: 44*

1 cup creamy peanut butter
1 cup sugar
1 teaspoon vanilla extract
1 large egg
2 cups semisweet chocolate morsels
Garnish: finely chopped salted peanuts

- Preheat oven to 350°.
- Line 2 rimmed baking sheets with parchment paper.
- In a medium bowl, combine peanut butter, sugar, vanilla extract, and egg. Beat at medium speed with an electric mixer until ingredients are incorporated.
- Using a levered 1-teaspoon scoop, divide dough into portions, and place 2 inches apart on prepared baking sheets. Using the bottom of a glass dipped in additional sugar, flatten cookies.
- Bake until cookies are puffed and set, approximately 8 minutes. Let cool on baking sheets for 1 to 2 minutes. Transfer to wire cooling racks, and let cool completely.
- In a small bowl, melt chocolate morsels according to package directions. Dip 1 end of cookies into melted chocolate, and place on a wire cooling rack.
- While chocolate is still wet, garnish with chopped peanuts, if desired. Let cool until chocolate is firm, approximately 2 hours.
- Store in between layers of waxed paper in an airtight container at room temperature for 2 to 3 days.

Fig Crumb Bars
Yield: 32

1 cup chopped dried figs
1 cup water
¾ cup plus 2 tablespoons quick-cooking oats
¾ cup plus 2 tablespoons all-purpose flour
½ cup firmly packed light brown sugar
½ teaspoon baking soda
½ cup cold salted butter
½ cup sugar
1 tablespoon plus ¼ teaspoon cornstarch
¼ teaspoon ground cinnamon
2 large egg yolks
¾ cup sour cream
1 teaspoon vanilla extract

- Preheat oven to 350°.
- Line an 8-inch square baking pan with a double thickness of parchment paper, letting edges of parchment paper hang over edges of pan. Spray with nonstick cooking spray.

Fig Crumb Bars

- In a small saucepan, combine figs and water. Bring to a boil, then reduce heat so that figs simmer slightly. Cook for 10 minutes. Drain figs well, and discard water.
- In a medium bowl, combine oats, flour, brown sugar, and baking soda, whisking well. Using a pastry blender, cut butter into oat mixture until crumbly. Continue to work mixture with hands, rubbing butter into oat mixture until mixture is uniformly moist. Press half of oat mixture into bottom of prepared pan, creating a level base. Reserve remaining half.
- Bake until light golden brown, approximately 7 minutes. Let cool.
- In a small saucepan, combine sugar, cornstarch, and cinnamon, whisking well. Add egg yolks, sour cream, and vanilla extract, whisking until incorporated. Cook over low heat until thickened and creamy (similar to pudding), approximately 3 minutes. Add figs, stirring to combine. Pour mixture into cooled crust. Crumble remaining half of oat mixture evenly over filling.
- Bake until set and golden brown, approximately 25 minutes. Let cool completely before cutting. Lift bars from pan, using parchment paper as handles. Cut into 2x1-inch bars.
- Serve at room temperature, or refrigerate overnight and serve cold.

Make-Ahead Tip: Make and bake bars a day in advance, cover, and refrigerate. Cut into bars while cold, and serve immediately or let come to room temperature.

"Friend is someone to share the last cookie with."

—The Cookie Monster, *Sesame Street*

Greek Easter Cookies (Koulourakia)
Yield: 58

1 cup salted butter, softened
1½ cups sugar
3 large eggs
½ teaspoon vanilla extract
¼ teaspoon almond extract
¼ teaspoon anise extract
1 tablespoon fresh orange zest
½ cup fresh orange juice
6 cups all-purpose flour
2 teaspoons baking powder
½ teaspoon baking soda
1 large egg, beaten
½ cup whole milk
3 tablespoons sesame seeds

• Preheat oven to 375°.
• Line several rimmed baking sheets with parchment paper. Set aside.
• In a large mixing bowl, combine butter and sugar. Beat at high speed with an electric mixer until light and fluffy, approximately 1 minute. Add eggs, one at a time, beating thoroughly after each addition. Add extracts, orange zest, and orange juice, beating to combine. (Mixture will appear curdled.)
• In a large bowl, combine flour, baking powder, and baking soda, whisking well. Add flour mixture to butter mixture in thirds. (Dough will be soft but not sticky.)
• Using a levered 1½-tablespoon scoop, divide dough into 58 portions. On a lightly floured surface and using hands, roll portions into 6x½-inch ropes. Fold each dough rope in half, and twist to form a braid. Place 2 inches apart on prepared baking sheets.
• In a small bowl, combine egg and milk, whisking well. Brush cookies with egg mixture, and sprinkle with sesame seeds.
• Bake until edges of cookies are light golden brown, approximately 10 minutes. Transfer to wire racks, and let cool completely.
• Store at room temperature in airtight containers to maintain cookies' soft breadlike texture.

Make-Ahead Tip: *Cookies can be baked in advance, placed in airtight containers, with layers separated by waxed paper, and frozen for up to 2 weeks. Let cookies thaw before serving.*

Ginger-Almond Cookies
Yield: 34 to 36

2 large egg whites
½ cup sugar
⅓ cup all-purpose flour
2 tablespoons minced crystallized ginger
3 tablespoons salted butter, melted and cooled
¼ cup sliced almonds

• Preheat oven to 400°.
• In a medium mixing bowl, beat egg whites at high speed with an electric mixer until stiff peaks form. Sprinkle sugar over egg whites, and fold in, using a spatula. Add flour and crystallized ginger, folding to combine. Add melted butter, folding to incorporate.
• Coat a baking sheet with butter and flour. Place prepared baking sheet in oven for 5 minutes.
• Drop batter by teaspoonfuls onto hot baking sheet. Working quickly and using an offset spatula, spread batter for each cookie thinly to silver-dollar size. Sprinkle cookies with almonds.
• Bake until cookies are light brown around edges, 2 to 4 minutes.
• Let cool briefly, approximately 1 minute, on baking sheet. Transfer to a wire rack, and let cool completely. (Cookies should have a crispy yet chewy texture.) Repeat baking-sheet preparation and procedure for remaining batches of cookies.
• Store at room temperature in an airtight container.

Greek Easter Cookies (Koulourakia)

Triple-Layer Brownies

Triple-Layer Brownies
Yield: 64

2½ cups dark chocolate morsels, divided
¾ cup salted butter, softened and divided
1¼ cups sugar
3 large eggs
1½ teaspoons vanilla extract, divided
1 cup all-purpose flour
¾ teaspoon salt, divided
1 cup creamy peanut butter
¾ cup confectioners' sugar
1 tablespoon whole milk
½ cup heavy whipping cream

- Preheat oven to 350°.
- Line a 9-inch square baking pan with heavy-duty foil. Spray foil with nonstick cooking spray.
- In a large microwave-safe bowl, combine 1½ cups chocolate morsels and ½ cup butter. Microwave for 1-minute intervals at 50 percent power, stirring to combine, until mixture is smooth.
- Add sugar, stirring to combine. Add eggs, one at a time, stirring well after each addition. Add ½ teaspoon vanilla extract, stirring well.
- In a small bowl, combine flour and ½ teaspoon salt, whisking well. Add to chocolate mixture, stirring to incorporate. Pour batter into prepared pan.
- Bake until a wooden pick inserted in the center comes out clean, 30 to 33 minutes. Let cool until slightly warm, approximately 15 minutes.
- In a medium bowl, combine peanut butter, remaining ¼ cup butter, confectioners' sugar, remaining ¼ teaspoon salt, milk, and remaining 1 teaspoon vanilla extract, stirring until blended.
- While brownie layer is slightly warm, use an offset spatula to spread peanut butter mixture over top in a smooth layer.
- In a small saucepan, heat cream until almost boiling. Remove from heat, and add remaining 1 cup chocolate morsels, stirring until smooth. Pour over peanut butter layer, spreading into a smooth layer. Refrigerate until chocolate layer becomes firm, 2 to 4 hours.
- Using edges of foil as handles, lift whole brownie from pan. Carefully remove foil, and place brownie on a cutting board. Using a long chef's knife, score chocolate ganache into 1-inch squares. To cut into individual brownies, line up knife with scored lines, pressing down firmly in one motion.
- Refrigerate, covered, for up to 3 days.

Strawberry French Madeleines
Yield: 48

1 cup all-purpose flour
1 teaspoon baking powder
⅛ teaspoon salt
4 large eggs
¾ cup sugar
2 teaspoons strawberry extract
½ cup salted butter, melted and cooled
Garnish: confectioners' sugar

- Preheat oven to 350°.
- Spray 4 (12-well) madeleine pans with nonstick baking spray with flour.
- In a small bowl, combine flour, baking powder, and salt.
- In a large mixing bowl, combine eggs, sugar, and strawberry extract. Beat at high speed with an electric mixer until pale and fluffy, approximately 5 minutes. Gradually add half of flour mixture to egg mixture, beating at medium speed until incorporated. Slowly add butter, beating until well blended. Add remaining flour mixture, beating until incorporated. Let batter stand for 5 minutes.
- Spoon 1 tablespoon batter into each prepared pan, smoothing with fingertip to create a level surface.
- Bake until light golden, approximately 5 minutes. Remove madeleines from molds, and let cool completely on wire racks.
- Dust with confectioners' sugar, if desired.

Make-Ahead Tip: *Strawberry French Madeleines can be made ahead and frozen (ungarnished) in an airtight container for up to 1 week. Let thaw before dusting with confectioners' sugar.*

Strawberry French Madelines

Lemon-Pistachio Shortbread

Lemon-Pistachio Shortbread

Yield: 36

1 cup plus 1 teaspoon salted butter, softened and divided
¼ cup firmly packed light brown sugar
½ cup confectioners' sugar
1 tablespoon fresh lemon zest
½ teaspoon lemon extract
2 cups all-purpose flour
¼ teaspoon salt
¼ cup finely chopped, roasted pistachios, divided

- Preheat oven to 300°.
- Butter an 8-inch square baking pan with 1 teaspoon butter.
- In a large mixing bowl, combine remaining 1 cup butter, brown sugar, confectioners' sugar, lemon zest, and lemon extract. Beat at high speed with an electric mixer until light and creamy, 2 to 3 minutes.
- In a medium bowl, combine flour and salt, whisking well. Add to butter mixture, beating until incorporated.
- Reserve 2 teaspoons chopped pistachios, and add remainder to dough, stirring well.
- Press dough evenly into prepared pan*. Using a sharp knife, lightly score 36 squares on dough. Sprinkle reserved pistachios over dough.
- Bake until shortbread is pale brown and firm, approximately 50 minutes. Let cool, then cut along scored lines.
- Store in an airtight container.

*To prevent sticking, use latex gloves or lightly dampen hands with water while pressing.

Lemon-Lavender Shortbread

Yield: 32 to 36

1 cup salted butter, softened
¼ cup firmly packed light brown sugar
½ cup confectioners' sugar
1 tablespoon fresh lemon zest
1½ teaspoons lemon extract
2 cups all-purpose flour
1 teaspoon dried culinary lavender
¼ teaspoon salt

- Preheat oven to 300°.
- Line an 8-inch square baking pan with a double thickness of parchment paper, letting paper hang over sides. Spray with nonstick cooking spray. Set aside.
- In a large mixing bowl, combine butter, brown sugar, confectioners' sugar, lemon zest, and lemon extract. Beat at medium-high speed with an electric mixer until light and creamy, 2 to 3 minutes. Set aside.
- In a medium bowl, combine flour, lavender, and salt, whisking well. Add to butter mixture, beating until incorporated. Press dough evenly into prepared pan*.
- Bake until shortbread is light golden brown, approximately 50 minutes. Place pan on a wire rack, and let cool completely.
- When cool, lift shortbread from pan, using parchment paper overhang as handles, and place on a cutting surface. Using a long, sharp knife, cut by pressing down to create clean cuts.
- Store in an airtight container until serving time.

*To prevent sticking, use latex gloves or lightly dampen hands with water while pressing.

Make-Ahead Tip: Lemon-Lavender Shortbread can be baked in advance, placed in an airtight container, and frozen for up to 2 weeks.

Lemon-Lavender Shortbread

Matcha French Macarons

Raspberry French Macarons

Macadamia–Vanilla Bean Macarons

Kitchen Tip: To measure confectioners' sugar accurately, spoon lightly into a measuring cup, and level off, using a straight edge. Do not pack or scoop sugar into cup as this will negatively affect final product.

Macadamia–Vanilla Bean Macarons
Gluten-free | *Yield: 24*

3 large egg whites
1 cup salted whole macadamia nuts
2 cups confectioners' sugar, divided (see Kitchen Tip on page 210)
1 vanilla bean, split lengthwise, seeds scraped and reserved
2 tablespoons granulated sugar
1 recipe White Chocolate–Lemon Ganache (recipe follows)

• Place egg whites in a medium mixing bowl, and let stand, uncovered, at room temperature for exactly 3 hours. (Aging the egg whites in this manner is essential to creating perfect macarons.)
• Line 2 rimmed baking sheets with parchment paper. Using a pencil, draw 1½-inch circles 2 inches apart on parchment paper. Turn parchment paper over.
• In the work bowl of a food processor, combine macadamia nuts and 1 tablespoon confectioners' sugar, pulsing until very finely ground. (Don't overprocess or you will create a nut butter. Nut particles should stay separate and dry, not clump together.) Add remaining confectioners' sugar and reserved vanilla bean seeds, and process just until combined.
• Beat egg whites at medium-high speed with an electric mixer until frothy. Gradually add granulated sugar, beating at high speed until stiff peaks form, 3 to 5 minutes. (Egg whites will be thick, creamy, and shiny.) Add macadamia nut mixture to egg whites, folding gently until well combined. Let batter stand for 15 minutes.
• Transfer batter to a piping bag fitted with a medium round tip (Wilton #12). Pipe batter onto drawn circles on prepared baking sheets. Slam baking sheets vigorously on countertop 5 to 7 times to release air bubbles. Let stand at room temperature for 45 to 60 minutes before baking to help develop the macaron's signature crisp exterior when baked. (Macarons should feel dry to the touch and should not stick to finger.)
• Preheat oven to 275°.
• Bake until firm to the touch, 23 to 24 minutes. Let cool completely on pans. Transfer to airtight containers. Refrigerate until ready to fill and serve.
• Place White Chocolate–Lemon Ganache in a pastry bag fitted with a medium round tip (Wilton #12). Pipe ganache onto flat side of macaron, and top with another macaron, flat sides together. Push down lightly and twist so that filling spreads to edges. Repeat with remaining macarons and filling.
• Serve immediately, or refrigerate in an airtight container for up to 3 days. Let come to room temperature before serving.

White Chocolate–Lemon Ganache
Gluten-free | *Yield: 1 cup*

2 (4-ounce) white chocolate baking bars
½ cup heavy whipping cream
1 tablespoon fresh lemon zest

• Finely chop white chocolate, and place in a medium bowl.
• In a small saucepan, heat cream over medium-high until very hot but not boiling. Pour hot cream over chocolate, and stir until chocolate melts and mixture is smooth. Add lemon zest, stirring to combine. Place bowl in a larger bowl filled with ice. Let cool, stirring often.

Raspberry French Macarons
Gluten-free | *Yield: 28*

3 large egg whites
¾ cup toasted slivered almonds*
2 cups confectioners' sugar (see Kitchen Tip on page 210)
½ cup freeze-dried raspberries
2 tablespoons granulated sugar
1 recipe Cream Cheese Filling (recipe on page 212)

• Place egg whites in a medium bowl, and let stand, uncovered, at room temperature for exactly 3 hours. (Aging the egg whites in this manner is essential to creating perfect French macarons.)
• Line several baking sheets with parchment paper. Using a pencil, draw 1½-inch circles 2 inches apart on parchment paper. Turn parchment paper over.
• In the work bowl of a food processor, combine almonds, 1 tablespoon confectioner's sugar, and raspberries, pulsing until very finely ground. (Don't overprocess, or you will create a nut butter. Nut particles should stay separate and dry but not clump together.) Add remaining confectioners' sugar, and process just until combined.
• Beat egg whites at medium-high speed with a mixer until frothy. Gradually add granulated sugar, beating at high speed until stiff peaks form, 3 to 5 minutes. (Egg whites will be thick, creamy, and shiny.) Add almond mixture to egg whites, folding gently by hand until well combined. Let batter stand for 15 minutes.
• Transfer batter to a pastry bag fitted with a medium round tip (Wilton #12). Pipe batter onto drawn circles on prepared baking sheets. Slam baking sheets vigorously on countertop 5 to 7 times to release air bubbles.
• Let stand at room temperature for 45 to 60 minutes before baking to help develop the macaron's signature crisp exterior when baked. (Macarons should feel dry to the touch and should not stick to finger.)
• Preheat oven to 275°.
• Bake until firm to the touch, approximately 22 minutes. Let cool completely on pans. Transfer to airtight containers. Refrigerate until ready to fill and serve.
• Place Cream Cheese Filling in a pastry bag fitted with a medium round tip (Wilton #12). Pipe filling onto flat side of macaron, and top with another macaron, flat sides together. Push down lightly and twist so that filling spreads to edges. Repeat with remaining macarons and filling.
• Serve immediately, or refrigerate in an airtight container for up to 3 days. Let come to room temperature before serving.

*We used Planters Recipe Ready Slivered Almonds.

Cream Cheese Filling
Gluten-free | Yield: 1 cup

1 (8-ounce) package cream cheese, softened
1 tablespoon heavy whipping cream
¼ teaspoon vanilla extract
⅓ cup confectioners' sugar

• In a small bowl, beat cream cheese and cream at medium speed with an electric mixer until smooth and creamy. Add vanilla extract and confectioners' sugar, beating until incorporated. Refrigerate in a covered container until needed.

Matcha French Macarons
Gluten-free | Yield: 24

3 large egg whites
1 cup toasted slivered almonds*
2 cups confectioners' sugar, divided (see Kitchen Tip on page 210)
1 tablespoon matcha powdered green tea
2 tablespoons granulated sugar
1 recipe Strawberry-Mascarpone Filling (recipe follows)

• Place egg whites in a medium bowl, and let stand, uncovered, at room temperature for exactly 3 hours. (Aging the egg whites in this manner is essential to creating perfect French macarons.)
• Line several baking sheets with parchment paper. Using a pencil, draw 1½-inch circles 2 inches apart on parchment paper. Turn parchment paper over.
• In the work bowl of a food processor, combine almonds, 1 tablespoon confectioners' sugar, and matcha tea, pulsing until very finely ground. (Don't overprocess, or you will create a nut butter. Nut particles should stay separate and dry but not clump together.) Add remaining confectioners' sugar, and process just until combined.
• Beat egg whites at medium-high speed with an electric mixer until frothy. Gradually add granulated sugar, beating at high speed until stiff peaks form, 3 to 5 minutes. (Egg whites will be thick, creamy, and shiny.) Add almond mixture to egg whites, folding gently by hand until well combined. Let batter stand for 15 minutes.
• Transfer batter to a pastry bag fitted with a medium round tip (Wilton #12). Pipe batter onto drawn circles on prepared baking sheets. Slam baking sheets vigorously on countertop 5 to 7 times to release air bubbles. Let stand at room temperature for 45 to 60 minutes before baking to help develop the macaron's signature crisp exterior when baked. (Macarons should feel dry to the touch and should not stick to finger.)
• Preheat oven to 275°.
• Bake until firm to the touch, approximately 22 minutes. Let cool completely on pans. Transfer to airtight containers. Refrigerate until ready to fill and serve.
• Place Strawberry-Mascarpone Filling in a pastry bag fitted with a medium round tip (Wilton #12). Pipe onto flat side of macaron, and top with another macaron, flat sides together. Push down lightly and twist so that filling spreads to edges. Repeat with remaining macarons and filling.
• Serve immediately, or refrigerate in an airtight container for up to 3 days. Let come to room temperature before serving.

*We used Planters Recipe Ready Slivered Almonds.

Strawberry-Mascarpone Filling
Gluten-free | Yield: 1½ cups

1 (8-ounce) container mascarpone cheese
½ cup strawberry preserves

• In a small bowl, combine mascarpone cheese and strawberry preserves, stirring until combined. Refrigerate in a covered container until cold, approximately 1 hour.

"Nothing is too much trouble if it turns out the way it should."

—Julia Child

Kitchen Tip: To measure nuts for macarons accurately, spoon lightly into a measuring cup, and level off, using a straight edge.

COOKIES AND BARS | *The Ultimate TeaTime Collection*

Make-Ahead Tip: *Cookies can be baked in advance, placed in an airtight container with layers separated by waxed paper, and frozen for up to 1 week. Let thaw completely before garnishing with confectioners' sugar.*

Stenciled Gingerbread Cookies

Stenciled Gingerbread Cookies
Yield: 40 to 42

3 cups all-purpose flour
3 teaspoons ground cinnamon
2 teaspoons ground ginger
½ teaspoon baking soda
½ teaspoon ground cloves
½ teaspoon salt
¼ teaspoon baking powder
¼ teaspoon ground nutmeg
⅛ teaspoon ground black pepper
½ cup salted butter, softened
½ cup firmly packed light brown sugar
½ cup molasses
1 large egg
Garnish: confectioners' sugar

- Preheat oven to 350°.
- Line several rimmed baking sheets with parchment paper. Set aside.
- In a large bowl, combine flour, cinnamon, ginger, baking soda, cloves, salt, baking powder, nutmeg, and pepper, whisking well.
- In a large mixing bowl, combine butter and brown sugar. Beat at medium speed with an electric mixer until well combined. Add molasses and egg, beating until incorporated. Add flour mixture, beating until a moist dough forms. Divide dough into 2 portions, and wrap each securely in plastic wrap. Refrigerate until dough is firm enough to roll out, approximately 1 hour.
- On a lightly floured surface, roll each dough portion to an ⅛-inch thickness. Using a 3-inch round scalloped-edge cutter, cut circles from dough, and place 2 inches apart on prepared pans. Reroll scraps as necessary.
- Bake for 8 minutes. Transfer cookies to wire racks, and let cool completely.
- When ready to serve, garnish with a dusting of confectioners' sugar, using a variety of stencils*, if desired.

*We used Martha Stewart Crafts stencils.

Apricot, Pistachio & Rosemary Biscotti
Yield: approximately 24

⅔ cup sugar
2 large eggs
1¼ teaspoons vanilla extract
1¾ cups all-purpose flour
1 teaspoon baking powder
1 teaspoon finely chopped fresh rosemary
¼ teaspoon salt
½ cup chopped, salted, roasted pistachios
½ cup finely chopped dried apricots

Apricot, Pistachio & Rosemary Biscotti

- Preheat oven to 350°.
- Line 2 rimmed baking sheets with parchment paper.
- In a large mixing bowl, combine sugar and eggs. Beat at high speed with an electric mixer until pale and fluffy, 3 to 5 minutes. Add vanilla extract, beating to blend.
- In a medium bowl, combine flour, baking powder, rosemary, and salt, whisking well. Add flour mixture to egg mixture, beating until incorporated. Add pistachios and apricots, beating at low speed just until incorporated.
- Turn dough out onto a floured surface. Using floured hands, roll into a 14-x-2-inch log shape. Place dough log on a prepared baking sheet.
- Bake until log is light brown and a wooden pick inserted in the center comes out clean, 25 to 30 minutes. (Log may crack during baking.) Transfer to a wire rack, and let cool until able to handle.
- Reduce oven temperature to 325°.
- Transfer log to a cutting surface. With a serrated knife, cut log diagonally into ¼-inch pieces, using a sawing motion. Lay slices flat on remaining prepared baking sheet.
- Bake for 6 to 8 minutes, turn slices over, and bake until light golden brown, an additional 8 to 10 minutes. Transfer slices to wire racks, and let cool completely.
- Store in airtight containers for up to 2 weeks.

Bonbon Cookies

- Using a levered 1-tablespoon scoop, divide dough into portions. Press nuts or dried fruit into dough while still in scoop, then drop 1 inch apart onto prepared baking sheets, rounded side up.
- Bake until set but not brown, 11 to 12 minutes. Remove cookies from baking sheets, and let cool completely on wire racks.
- In a medium bowl, combine remaining 1 cup confectioners' sugar, milk, and remaining 1 teaspoon vanilla extract, whisking until completely smooth. Divide into 2 equal portions. Tint 1 portion with pink food coloring and the other with green food coloring. Dip tops of cookies into tinted icing. Dry, icing side up, on wire racks.
- Store at room temperature in an airtight container.

Make-Ahead Tip: Bonbon Cookies can be made in advance and frozen (unglazed) in an airtight container for up to 1 week. Let thaw before glazing.

Orange Marmalade Thumbprint Cookies
Yield: 48

2¼ cups all-purpose flour
1 teaspoon baking powder
¼ teaspoon salt
1 cup salted butter, softened
⅔ cup sugar
2 large egg yolks
1 tablespoon fresh orange zest
1 tablespoon fresh orange juice
1 teaspoon vanilla extract
½ cup orange marmalade

Bonbon Cookies
Yield: 26 to 28

1½ cups confectioners' sugar, divided
½ cup salted butter, softened
3 tablespoons light brown sugar
1 tablespoon heavy whipping cream
3½ teaspoons vanilla extract, divided
½ teaspoon almond extract
1½ cups all-purpose flour
⅛ teaspoon salt
Toasted nuts (such as macadamias or cashews) or dried fruit (such as cherries or apricots)
2 tablespoons whole milk
Pink and green gel food coloring

- Preheat oven to 350°.
- Line 2 baking sheets with parchment paper.
- In a medium bowl, combine ½ cup confectioners' sugar, butter, brown sugar, cream, 2½ teaspoons vanilla extract, and almond extract, stirring until smooth. Add flour and salt, stirring until incorporated. (If dough seems dry, add more cream, 1 tablespoon at a time, until a dough forms.)

- Preheat oven to 350°.
- Line 2 baking sheets with parchment paper.
- In a medium bowl, combine flour, baking powder, and salt, whisking well.
- In a large mixing bowl, combine butter and sugar. Beat at medium speed with an electric mixer until light and creamy. Add egg yolks, orange zest, orange juice, and vanilla extract, beating to combine. Add flour mixture to egg mixture in 2 portions, beating until moist clumps form. Gather dough into a ball.
- Shape dough into 1-inch balls. Place 1 inch apart on prepared baking sheets.
- Using a floured finger or a ½-teaspoon measuring spoon, make a depression in the center of each ball. Divide marmalade among depressions (½ teaspoon each).
- Bake until golden brown, 15 to 20 minutes. Transfer cookies to wire racks, and let cool completely.
- Store cookies in an airtight container in the refrigerator.

Make-Ahead Tip: Orange Marmalade Thumbprint Cookies can be made ahead and frozen for up to 1 week. Let thaw before serving.

Key Lime Bars

Orange Marmalade Thumbprint Cookies

Key Lime Bars
Yield: 32

½ cup salted butter, softened
1¼ cups sugar, divided
1½ cups all-purpose flour, divided
⅛ teaspoon salt
3 large eggs
1 tablespoon fresh lime zest
⅓ cup Key lime juice*
Garnish: confectioners' sugar

• Preheat oven to 350°.
• Line an 8-inch square baking pan with aluminum foil, leaving a 1-inch overhang on all sides.
• In a medium mixing bowl, combine butter and ¼ cup sugar. Beat at high speed with an electric mixer until light and creamy.
• In a small bowl, combine 1 cup flour and salt, whisking well. Add flour mixture to butter mixture, stirring until incorporated.
• Using floured hands, press dough into the bottom of prepared baking pan, building up a ½-inch edge on all sides.
• Bake until light golden brown, approximately 15 minutes. Let cool.
• In another bowl, combine eggs, remaining 1 cup sugar, lime zest, lime juice, and remaining ½ cup flour, whisking well. Pour over cooled crust.
• Bake until filling is set, approximately 30 minutes. Let cool to room temperature.
• Using aluminum foil as handles, remove dessert from pan. Trim away sides of crust, if desired. Cut dessert into 32 (2x1-inch) bars.
• Garnish with a dusting of confectioners' sugar, if desired.

*Fresh lime juice may be substituted, but the flavor will not be as tart.

Other Sweets

CHOCOLATE TRUFFLE CONES WITH JASMINE WHIPPED CREAM
(recipe on page 224)

Pecan Meringue Drops

Pecan Meringue Drops
Yield: approximately 32

3 large egg whites, at room temperature
¼ teaspoon cream of tartar
½ cup sugar
¼ cup confectioners' sugar
1 teaspoon vanilla extract
⅛ teaspoon salt
⅓ cup finely chopped toasted pecans*

• Preheat oven to 250°.
• Line several rimmed baking pans with parchment paper.
• In a large mixing bowl, combine egg whites and cream of tartar. Beat at high speed with an electric mixer until soft peaks begin to form. Add sugars, vanilla extract, and salt, beating until incorporated. Continue to beat at high speed until stiff peaks form and meringue is shiny, approximately 3 minutes. Reduce mixer speed to low, and add chopped pecans, beating until incorporated.
• Transfer mixture to a piping bag fitted with a very large open-star tip (Ateco #848). Pipe drops onto prepared baking pans.
• Bake for 1 hour. Turn oven off, and let sit overnight in oven with door closed. (This will help meringues dry out and form a lightly airy texture.) The next day, store at room temperature in an airtight container.

*Make sure pecans are chopped finely enough to pass through a piping tip.

Kitchen Tip: Anchor parchment sheets to baking pans by piping small dots of meringue mixture at corners before placing parchment sheet on pan. This will keep paper in place while piping meringues. Pipe meringue onto parchment paper, pulling tip up to form a drop shape.

Make-Ahead Tip: Meringues can be made several days in advance and stored at room temperature in an airtight container.

Éclairs
Yield: 24

¾ cup water
6 tablespoons salted butter, cubed, at room temperature
2 teaspoons sugar
¼ teaspoon salt
¾ cup all-purpose flour
3 large eggs, at room temperature
1 recipe Vanilla Pastry Cream (recipe follows)
1 recipe Chocolate Glaze (recipe follows)

• Preheat oven to 400°.
• Line 2 rimmed baking sheets with silicone baking mats or parchment paper.
• In a medium saucepan, combine water, butter, sugar, and salt. Cook over medium heat until butter melts. Add flour all at once, stirring vigorously with a wooden spoon. Cook and stir until dough pulls away from sides of pan, 1 to 2 minutes. Remove pan from heat, and let stand for 2 minutes, stirring a few times to cool dough.
• Add eggs, one at a time, stirring constantly and vigorously with a wooden spoon until each egg is well incorporated. (Dough should be smooth and shiny.) Transfer dough to a resealable plastic bag with a corner snipped off to make a ½-inch opening. Pipe dough onto prepared baking sheets in 3-inch lengths, spacing 1 inch apart.
• Bake until golden brown, approximately 15 minutes. Let cool completely before filling.
• Using a serrated knife, cut éclair shells in half lengthwise. Place Vanilla Pastry Cream in a resealable plastic bag with a corner snipped off to make a ½-inch opening. Pipe pastry cream onto bottom halves of shells. Top with remaining halves of éclair shells. Set aside.
• Place Chocolate Glaze in a piping bag, and snip off tip of bag. Pipe glaze on top of éclairs.
• Serve immediately, or refrigerate for up to 2 hours before serving.

Make-Ahead Tip: Éclair shells can be made in advance and frozen (unfilled) in an airtight container for up to a week. Let thaw completely before filling.

Éclairs

Vanilla Pastry Cream
Yield: 1¾ cups

4 large egg yolks
½ cup sugar
2 cups whole milk
3 tablespoons cornstarch
⅛ teaspoon salt
1 tablespoon butter
1½ teaspoons vanilla extract

• In a medium bowl, combine egg yolks and sugar, whisking well.
• In a medium saucepan, heat milk to very hot but not boiling. Add hot milk, ¼ cup at a time, to eggs to temper, whisking constantly. Add cornstarch and salt, whisking until incorporated. Strain mixture through a fine-mesh sieve.
• Return mixture to saucepan, and cook over medium heat, whisking constantly until mixture thickens. Remove from heat, and add butter and vanilla extract, whisking until incorporated.
• Transfer pastry cream to a heatproof bowl. Cover with plastic wrap, letting plastic touch surface of custard. Refrigerate until pastry cream is very cold, 4 to 6 hours or overnight.

Chocolate Glaze
Yield: ⅔ cup

½ cup heavy whipping cream
1 (4-ounce) bar semisweet chocolate, very finely chopped

• In a small saucepan, heat cream almost to boiling. Remove pan from heat, and add chocolate, stirring until chocolate melts and mixture is smooth. Let cool slightly until somewhat thickened before using.

Caramel Cream Puffs

Caramel Cream Puffs
Yield: 24

¾ cup water
6 tablespoons salted butter, cut into pieces
2 teaspoons sugar
¼ teaspoon salt
¾ cup all-purpose flour
3 large eggs, at room temperature
1 (8-ounce) container mascarpone cheese
½ cup dulce de leche*
Garnish: confectioners' sugar

- Preheat oven to 400°.
- Line 2 rimmed baking sheets with silicone baking mats or parchment paper.
- In a medium saucepan, combine water, butter, sugar, and salt. Cook over medium heat until butter melts. Add flour all at once, stirring vigorously with a wooden spoon. Cook, and stir until dough pulls away from sides of pan, 1 to 2 minutes. Remove pan from heat, and let stand for 2 minutes, stirring a few times to cool dough.
- Add eggs, one at a time, stirring constantly and vigorously with a wooden spoon until each egg is well incorporated. (Dough should be smooth and shiny.) Transfer dough to a piping bag fitted with a large round tip (Ateco #809). Pipe dough onto prepared baking sheet in 1½-inch mounds, spacing 1 inch apart. Pat dough peaks down with a damp finger.
- Bake until golden brown, approximately 20 minutes. Transfer baking sheet to a wire rack. Using a skewer or the tip of a pointed knife, poke a small hole in side of each cream puff to allow steam to escape. Let cool completely.
- In a medium bowl, combine mascarpone and dulce de leche, stirring until smooth and creamy. Transfer mixture to a piping bag fitted with a large open-star tip (Wilton #1M). Set aside.
- Using a serrated knife, cut each cream puff in half horizontally. Pipe caramel mixture in a decorative swirl onto bottom halves of cream puffs. Top with remaining halves.
- Garnish with a sifting of confectioners' sugar, if desired.
- Serve immediately.

*Dulche de leche is a caramel spread available in the canned milk section of most grocery stores.

Make-Ahead Tip: *Cream puffs can be made a week in advance and frozen (unfilled) in heavy-duty resealable plastic bags. Let thaw completely before filling.*

Blackberry-Buttermilk Sherbet

Blackberry-Buttermilk Sherbet
Gluten-free | *Yield: 9 (⅓-cup) servings*

1 (10-ounce) jar seedless blackberry preserves*
2 cups cold whole buttermilk
1 vanilla bean, split lengthwise, seeds scraped and reserved
¼ teaspoon ground black pepper
⅛ teaspoon salt
Garnish: edible flowers†

- In a medium bowl, whisk preserves until loosened and smooth. Add buttermilk, reserved vanilla bean seeds, pepper, and salt, stirring to combine. Pour mixture into a 1½-quart countertop ice-cream maker. Freeze according to manufacturer's directions. (This should take approximately 25 minutes.)
- Transfer sherbet to an airtight container, cover surface with plastic wrap, and freeze until ready to serve.
- Garnish individual servings with edible flowers, if desired.

*It's important to use high-quality blackberry preserves to create a fresh blackberry taste.

†We used edible flowers from Gourmet Sweet Botanicals, gourmetsweetbotanicals.com.

Kitchen Tip: *Ground black pepper may seem to be an unusual ingredient for ice cream, but it provides a counterpoint to the sweetness of the sherbet.*

Chocolate Truffle Cones with Jasmine Whipped Cream

Chocolate Truffle Cones with Jasmine Whipped Cream
Yield: 6

1½ cups heavy whipping cream, divided
2 bags jasmine green tea
2 tablespoons confectioners' sugar
¾ cup semisweet chocolate morsels
6 waffle cones
½ cup fresh blueberries
½ cup fresh raspberries
Garnish: sugar pearls, nonpareils, pearlized jimmies, luster flakes

- In a small saucepan, heat 1 cup cream until very hot but not boiling. (Bubbles should appear around the edges of pan.) Remove from heat, and add tea bags. Let steep for 10 minutes; remove and discard tea bags. Refrigerate infused cream in a covered container until very cold, 8 hours or overnight.
- In a large bowl, combine cold infused cream and confectioners' sugar. Beat at high speed with an electric mixer until stiff peaks form. Cover, and refrigerate until serving time.
- In a small saucepan, heat remaining ½ cup cream until very hot but not boiling. Remove from heat, and add chocolate morsels, stirring until chocolate melts and mixture is smooth. Pour melted chocolate into a heatproof bowl. Set bowl in a bowl of crushed ice to cool, stirring occasionally. When chocolate is the consistency of cake frosting, place in a resealable plastic bag with a corner snipped off to make a ½-inch opening.
- Place waffle cones on a cutting board, and using a sharp serrated knife, carefully cut off and discard approximately 2 inches of cone top, leaving a 4-inch length of cone.
- Divide blueberries and raspberries among waffle cones. Pipe chocolate mixture over fruit to fill cones. At this point, cones can be placed in a covered container and refrigerated for up to 2 hours before serving.
- Just before serving, transfer jasmine whipped cream to a piping bag fitted with a large open-star tip (Wilton #1M). Pipe a decorative rosette onto tops of cones.
- Garnish with sugar pearls, nonpareils, jimmies, and luster flakes, if desired.

Kitchen Tip: *To make waffle cones easier to fill and refrigerate, stand each one up in a small juice glass.*

Coconut–Vanilla Bean Panna Cottas
Gluten-free | Yield: 6 (½-cup) servings

3 tablespoons water
1 (.25-ounce) envelope unflavored gelatin
1 cup heavy whipping cream
1 (13.5-ounce) can coconut milk
½ cup confectioners' sugar
¼ teaspoon salt
1 vanilla bean, split lengthwise, seeds scraped and reserved
¼ teaspoon coconut extract
Garnish: fresh edible flowers*

- Place 6 teacups or 6 (½-cup) ramekins on a rimmed baking sheet.
- Place water in a small bowl. Sprinkle gelatin over water, and let stand for 10 minutes.
- In a medium saucepan, combine cream, coconut milk, confectioners' sugar, salt, and reserved vanilla-bean seeds, whisking well. Cook over medium-high heat until very hot but not boiling. Remove from heat, and add gelatin mixture, whisking until incorporated. Add coconut extract. Let mixture cool slightly so that it will not shatter delicate teacups.
- Divide cream mixture evenly among teacups, whisking frequently so vanilla-bean seeds do not settle at bottom.
- Cover with plastic wrap, not letting plastic wrap touch surface of cream mixture. Refrigerate until set, approximately 4 hours.
- Garnish each serving with fresh edible flowers, if desired.

*We used edible flowers from Gourmet Sweet Botanicals, gourmetsweetbotanicals.com.

Kitchen Tip: *Transfer cream mixture to a liquid measuring cup with a pouring spout to make it easier to pour into teacups.*

Make-Ahead Tip: *Panna cottas can be made a day in advance. Cover teacups with plastic wrap, but don't let wrap touch surface of panna cottas.*

Coconut–Vanilla Bean Panna Cottas

Brown Sugar–Cashew Fudge

Brown Sugar–Cashew Fudge
Gluten-free | Yield: approximately 49 pieces

⅔ cup evaporated milk
2 cups firmly packed light brown sugar
¾ cup salted butter, cut into chunks
⅛ teaspoon salt
1 teaspoon vanilla extract
1¾ cups confectioners' sugar
1 (7-ounce) jar marshmallow crème
1 cup finely chopped roasted, salted cashews

- Line an 8-inch square pan with heavy-duty aluminum foil. Spray foil with nonstick cooking spray.
- In a heavy medium saucepan, combine milk, brown sugar, butter, and salt. Bring to a boil over medium-high heat, stirring constantly. Reduce heat to medium, and cook for 5 minutes, stirring frequently. Remove pan from heat, and add vanilla extract.
- Using an electric mixer, gradually add confectioners' sugar, beating until smooth and creamy. Add marshmallow crème, stirring quickly and vigorously with a wooden spoon until incorporated. Add cashews, stirring to combine.
- Spread mixture into prepared pan, smoothing to create an even layer. Let stand for several hours until fudge is firm enough to cut.
- Lift fudge from pan, using foil as handles, and place on a cutting surface. Using a long, sharp knife, press downward to create clean cuts.
- Store fudge in an airtight container at room temperature.

Kiwi, Mango & Coconut Pavlovas

Kiwi, Mango & Coconut Pavlovas
Gluten-free | Yield: 10

2 large egg whites, at room temperature
¼ teaspoon cream of tartar
⅛ teaspoon salt
½ cup sugar
2 ounces cream cheese, softened
¼ cup sour cream
¼ cup firmly packed light brown sugar
¼ teaspoon vanilla extract
2⅓ cups sliced kiwi
⅔ cup diced mango
¼ cup toasted coconut

- Preheat oven to 250°.
- Line a baking sheet with parchment paper. Using a 3-inch round cutter and a pencil, trace 10 circles, 2 inches apart, onto parchment. Turn parchment over so pencil marks are face down on baking sheet.
- In a medium mixing bowl, combine egg whites, cream of tartar, and salt. Beat at high speed with an electric mixer until soft peaks form. Add sugar gradually while beating until stiff peaks form. (Meringue mixture will look glossy.) Transfer mixture to a piping bag fitted with a medium open-star tip (Wilton #21).
- Starting in the middle of each traced circle, pipe concentric circles of meringue mixture outward until circle is filled. Pipe 1 to 2 extra layers on perimeters of rounds to form a rim around the edge of each circle.
- Bake for 1 hour. Turn off oven, and let sit in oven for at least 2 hours or overnight. (This will help meringues continue to dry and form a crispy shell.)
- In a small bowl, combine cream cheese, sour cream, brown sugar, and vanilla extract, beating at medium speed with an electric mixer until mixture is smooth and creamy. Cover, and refrigerate until ready to use.
- Divide cream cheese mixture evenly among meringue shells. Arrange kiwi slices in shells, overlapping and curving to form a flower shape. Place diced mango in center of each, and sprinkle with toasted coconut. Serve immediately.

How-Tos

Let these step-by-step instructions serve as your visual guide while you create these impressive and delicious teatime treats.

BASIC SCONES

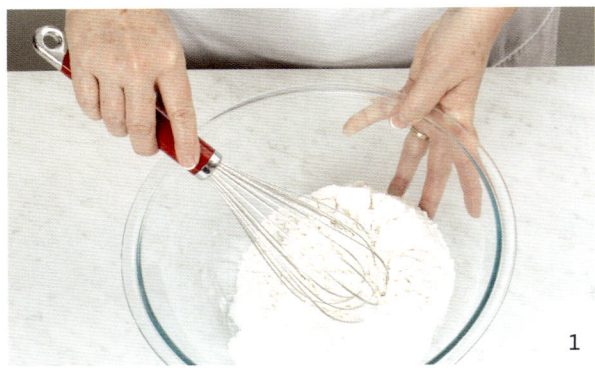

1. In a large bowl, combine the dry ingredients, whisking well.

2. Using a pastry blender, cut cold butter into flour mixture until mixture resembles coarse crumbs.

3. If the recipe calls for dried fruit, nuts, chocolate, or other additions, add them at this point, tossing to combine.

4. Add wet ingredients to flour mixture, stirring until mixture is evenly moist.

5

Working gently, bring mixture together with hands until a dough forms.

6

Turn out dough onto a lightly floured surface. Knead gently 4 to 5 times.

7

Using a rolling pin, roll dough to thickness indicated in recipe, usually ½ to 1 inch.

8

Using a cutter, cut scones from dough. Place scones 2 inches apart on a baking sheet lined with parchment paper.

9

If the recipe calls for it, brush tops of scones with cream.

10

Bake until edges of scones are golden brown and a wooden pick inserted in the centers comes out clean.

FRESH FRUIT SCONES

Prepare dough according to Steps 1–6 of Basic Scones How-to on pages 228–229, and then follow these steps before baking:

7

Using a rolling pin, roll dough to a ½-inch thickness.

8

Scatter half of the fruit over half of the dough. Fold remaining half of the dough over the fruit half.

9

Gently roll dough to a ½-inch thickness again.

10

Scatter remaining fruit over half the dough, and fold remaining half of the dough over the fruit again.

11

Gently roll dough to thickness indicated in recipe, usually ½ to 1 inch.

12

Using a cutter, cut scones from dough, gently rerolling scraps as needed. Place scones 2 inches apart on a baking sheet lined with parchment paper.

CHECKERBOARD HERBED BUTTER TEA SANDWICHES

1

Arrange 3 bread rectangles, long sides together, alternating pumpernickel and rye. Spread a thick layer of herbed butter on top.

2

Place 3 more bread rectangles on top, alternating rye and pumpernickel.

3

Spread another layer of herbed butter on top. Finish with 3 more bread rectangles, alternating pumpernickel and rye.

4

Just before serving, using a serrated bread knife in a gentle sawing motion, cut sandwiches crossways into ½-inch slices.

MANGO CHUTNEY–CUCUMBER FLOWER CANAPÉS

1

Fold very thin slices of cucumber in half, and fold again into quarters.

2

Place on prepared canapés with point facing the center.

3

Add four more folded cucumber slices, letting them unfold slightly to resemble the petals of a flower.

TARTLET CRUST

1

Using a cutter, cut shapes from dough.

2

Press dough shapes into tartlet pans.

3

Trim excess dough.

4

Using the wide end of a chopstick, push dough into indentations of pan.

GREEK EASTER COOKIES

1

Divide dough into 1½-tablespoon portions.

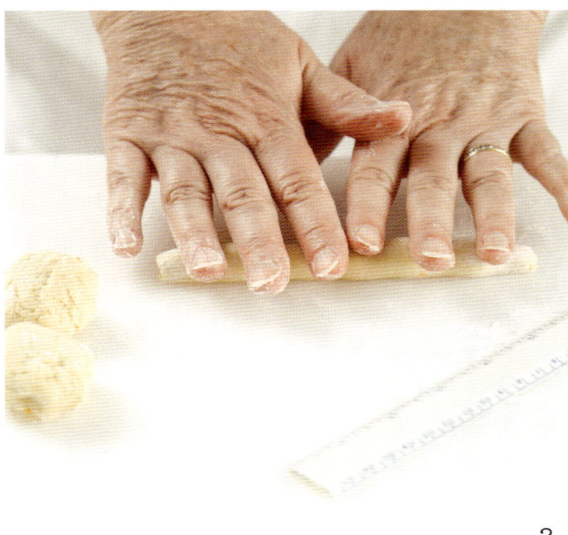

2

On a lightly floured surface, roll portions of dough to 6-x-½-inch ropes.

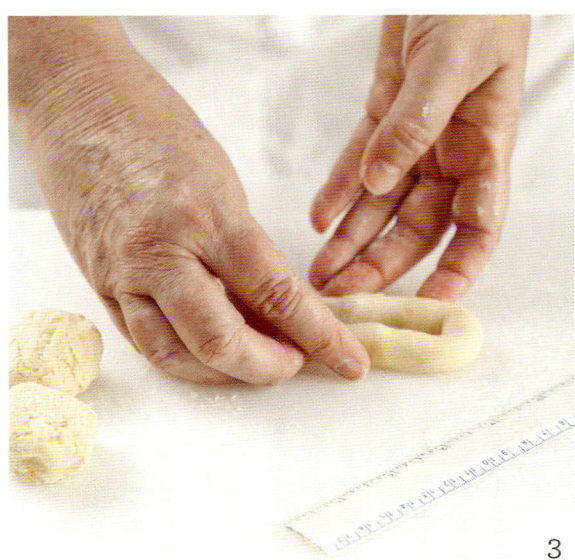

3

Fold each dough rope in half.

4

Twist rope to form a braid.

PEACH-GINGER TARTLETS

1

Using a paring knife, cut peach halves into ¼-inch slices.

2

Arrange longest slices around outer edges of tartlets, overlapping ends.

3

Add more slices to make a flower shape.

4

Brush tartlets with reserved heavy syrup.

PAVLOVAS

1. Line a baking sheet with parchment paper. Trace 2-inch circles onto parchment. Flip parchment over.

2. Working from the center outward, pipe concentric circles of meringue mixture until circle is filled.

3. Pipe 1 to 2 extra layers onto perimeters of rounds to form a rim around the edge of each circle.

4. Repeat piping procedure to fill all traced circles. Bake according to recipe.

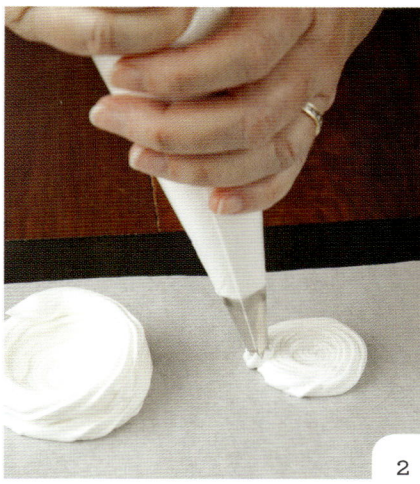

STRAWBERRY ROSETTES

1. Using a pairing knife, make 2 intersecting cuts in each strawberry, keeping the base intact.

2. On each quarter of the strawberry, make a small cut, angling the knife slightly inward.

Acknowledgments

COVER
Minton *Marlow* 5-piece place setting, 3-tiered serving tray, and teapot from Replacements, Ltd., 800-737-5223, *replacements.com*. Sferra *Festival* dinner napkins in *Hydrangea*, 877-336-2003, *sferra.com*.

TITLE PAGE
Page 2: *Blue Danube* teapot, cup and saucer, and salad plate from Replacements, Ltd., 800-737-5223, *replacements.com*.

MASTHEAD
Pages 4–5: Royal Albert *Lady Carlyle* teapot, cups and saucers, and salad plates from Replacements, Ltd., 800-737-5223, *replacements.com*. Maryland China Company Bernadotte gold-edged 3-tier tidbit tray, 800-638-3880, *marylandchina.com*. Heritage Lace *Canterbury Classic* table topper, 641-628-4949, *heritagelace.com*.

INTRODUCTION
Page 8: Bernardaud *Eden Turquoise* dinner plate and cup and saucer from Bromberg's, 205-871-3276, *brombergs.com*. Minton *Riverton* teapot from Replacements, Ltd., 800-737-5223, *replacements.com*.

TEA-STEEPING GUIDE
Pages 10–11: Haviland *Galaxy* bread and butter plate, teapot, and cup and saucer from Replacements, Ltd., 800-737-5223, *replacements.com*.

TEA-PAIRING GUIDE
Pages 12–13: Royal Albert *Old Country Roses* cup and saucer; Royal Crown Derby *Heraldic Gold* teapot from Replacements, Ltd., 800-737-5223, *replacements.com*. Heritage Lace *Canterbury Classic* table topper, 641-628-4949, *heritagelace.com*.

PLAIN SCONES
Page 18: Emile Henry *Ruffle Sky* platter, 302-326-4800, *emilehenryusa.com*. **Page 19:** Staffordshire *Calico Blue* accent salad plate from Replacements, Ltd., 800-737-5223, *replacements.com*.

SWEET SCONES
Page 22: Raynaud *Allée Royale* dinner plate, bread-and-butter plate, teacup, and saucer from Bromberg's, 205-871-3276, *brombergs.com*. **Page 23:** Anna Weatherly *Spring in Budapest* salad plate and *Simply Anna* cup and saucer from DeVine Corporation, 732-751-0500, *devinecorp.net*. **Page 24:** Royal Albert *Old Country Roses* salad plate and cup and saucer from Replacements, Ltd., 800-737-5223, *replacements.com*. **Page 25:** Minton *Marlow* 3-tiered serving tray from Replacements, Ltd., 800-737-5223, *replacements.com*. **Page 26:** Wedgwood *Colonnade Gold* salad plate and teapot with lid from Replacements, Ltd., 800-737-5223, *replacements.com*. **Page 28:** Haviland *Princess* salad plate, cup and saucer, and teapot from Replacements, Ltd., 800-737-5223, *replacements.com*. **Page 32:** Vietri *Incanto Lace* salad plate from Bromberg's, 205-871-3276, *brombergs.com*. Holiday spreaders from Mud Pie, 678-397-0170, *mud-pie.com*. **Page 33:** Crown Ducal *Bristol Pink* oversize teacup from Replacements, Ltd., 800-737-5223, *replacements.com*. **Page 34:** Spode *Stafford White* salad plate and cup and saucer from Replacements, Ltd., 800-737-5223, *replacements.com*. Bella Notte *Lavender* tea towel from Bromberg's, 205-871-3276, *brombergs.com*. **Page 36:** Smith Glass Co. *Trellis* cake stand in clear. **Page 38:** Gien *Filets Bleus* bread-and-butter plate, *www.gienshop.com*. **Page 39:** Lenox *Winter Greetings* salad plate and teapot from Replacements, Ltd., 800-737-5223, *replacements.com*. **Page 40:** Lenox *Holiday Tartan* bread-and-butter plate from Replacements, Ltd., 800-737-5223, *replacements.com*. **Page 41:** Royal Crown Derby *Brittany* dinner plate, salad plate, and cup and saucer from Replacements, Ltd., 800-737-5223, *replacements.com*. **Page 42:** Vietri *Incanto* baking dish and *Bellezza White* espresso cup and saucer from Bromberg's, 205-871-3276, *brombergs.com*. **Page 43:** Godinger China *Regal Cream* square dessert plate from Replacements, Ltd., 800-737-5223, *replacements.com*. **Page 44:** Bernardaud *Au Jardin* dinner plate, bread-and-butter plate, and teacup and saucer from Bromberg's, 205-871-3276, *brombergs.com*. **Page 45:** Wood tiered stand from Sur La Table, *surlatable.com*. **Page 48:** Wedgwood & Bentley *Dynasty Gold* 5-piece place setting; Waterford crystal tiered stand from Bromberg's, 205-871-3276, *brombergs.com*. **Page 50:** Vietri *Incanto White* striped bowl from Bromberg's, 205-871-3276, *brombergs.com*. Spode *Camilla Blue* teapot from Replacements, Ltd., 800-737-5223, *replacements.com*. **Page 51:** Annieglass *Roman Antique Gold* oval tray from Bromberg's, 205-871-3276, *brombergs.com*. Spode *Stafford White* salad plate and cup and saucer from Replacements, Ltd., 800-737-5223, *replacements.com*. **Page 53:** Johnson Brothers *Eternal Beau* 5-piece place setting from Replacements, Ltd., 800-737-5223, *replacements.com*.

GLUTEN-FREE SCONES
Page 56: Spode *Indian Tree-Orange/Rust* salad plate and footed cup and saucer from Replacements, Ltd., 800-737-5223, *replacements.com*. **Page 57:** Herend *Royal Garden* salad plate from Bromberg's, 205-871-3276, *brombergs.com*. **Page 58:** Bernardaud *Saison* dinner plate, salad plate, and cup and saucer from Bromberg's, 205-871-3276, *brombergs.com*. **Page 60:** Spode *Stafford White* salad plate and cup and saucer from Replacements, Ltd., 800-737-5223, *replacements.com*. **Page 61:** Royal Crown Derby *India* salad plate and teacup and saucer from Bromberg's, 205-871-3276, *brombergs.com*.

DELECTABLE SPREADS
Page 64: Juliska *Berry & Thread* Bowl from Bromberg's, 205-871-3276, *brombergs.com*. Vietri *Bellezza White* espresso cup and saucer from Bromberg's, 205-871-3276, *brombergs.com*. **Page 66:** Juliska *Berry & Thread* Bowl from Bromberg's, 205-871-3276, *brombergs.com*. **Page 67:** Haviland *Princess* dinner plate and cup and saucer from Replacements, Ltd., 800-737-5223, *replacements.com*. **Page 68:** Anthropologie *Fleur De Lys* salad plate, 800-309-2500, *anthropologie.com*.

SOUPS AND SALADS
Page 75–76: Raynaud *Allée Royale* dinner plate and salad plate from DeVine Corporation, 732-751-0500, *devinecorp.net*. Pier1 gold charger, 800-245-4595, *pier1.com*. Juliska *Berry & Thread* Bowl from Bromberg's, 205-871-3276, *brombergs.com*. **Page 77:** Royal Albert *Lady Carlyle* cream soup bowl from Replacements, Ltd., 800-737-5223, *replacements.com*. **Page 78:** Royal Crown Derby *Titanic* 5-piece plate setting from Replacements, Ltd., 800-737-5223, *replacements.com*. Gorham *Strasbourg* salad fork from Bromberg's, 205-871-3276, *brombergs.com*. **Page 79:** Royal Winton *Summertime* salad plate and square dinner plate; Hazel Atlas *Royal Lace* cream soup bowl from Replacements, Ltd., 800-737-5223, *replacements.com*. **Page 80:** Villeroy & Boch *Wonderful World Orange* dinner plate from Replacements, Ltd., 800-737-5223, *replacements.com*. Pier1 mini dessert bowls, 800-245-4595, *pier1.com*. **Page 82:** Lenox Kate Spade New York *Bissell Cove* accent plate from Replacements, Ltd., 800-737-5223, *replacements.com*. **Page 83:** Aynsley *Pembroke* cream soup bowls from Replacements, Ltd., 800-737-5223, *replacements.com*. Heritage Lace *Newport* table runner, 641-628-4949, *heritagelace.com*. **Page 84:** Villeroy & Boch *Persia* cream soup bowl, 800-845-5376, *villeroy-boch.com*. **Page 85:** Aynsley *Pembroke* crescent salad plate from Replacements, Ltd., 800-737-5223, *replacements.com*. **Page 86:** Bernardaud *Artois Green* 5-piece place setting from Replacements, Ltd., 800-737-5223, *replacements.com*. **Page 87:** Maryland China Company *Bernadotte* gold-edged 3-tier tidbit tray, 800-638-3880, *marylandchina.com*. **Page 88:** Wedgwood *Ascot* dinner plate and salad plate from Replacements, Ltd., 800-737-5223, *replacements.com*. Juliska *Colette* dessert bowl from Bromberg's, 205-871-3276, *brombergs.com*. **Page 89:** Wedgwood *Charnwood* cups and saucers from Replacements, Ltd., 800-737-5223, *replacements.com*. Heritage Lace *Grantham* runner, 641-628-4949, *heritagelace.com*. **Page 90:** Marchesa by Lenox *Spring Lark* 5-piece place setting, 800-223-4311, *lenox.com*. World Market fluted silver chargers, 877-967-5362, *worldmarket.com*. Patricia Spratt *Whisper Paisley* tablecloth, 860-434-9291, *patriciaspratforthehome.com*. Juliska *Berry & Thread* glass bowl from Bromberg's, 205-871-3276, *brombergs.com*. **Page 91:** Wedgwood *Osborne* cream soup bowl, 877-720-3486, *wedgwoodusa.com*.

QUICHES AND TARTLETS
Page 97: Royal Worcester *Regency Blue* dinner plate and salad plate from Replacements, Ltd., 800-737-5223, *replacements.com*. **Page 98:** Vietri *Lastra White* handled rectangular platter, 919-245-4180, *vietri.com*. **Page 99:** White classic lace napkins, 800-243-0852, *surlatable.com*. **Page 100:** Lenox *French Perle White* hors d'oeuvres tray, 800-223-4311, *lenox.com*. **Page 101:** Maryland China Company *Bernadotte* gold-edged 3-tier tidbit tray, 800-638-3880, *marylandchina.com*. **Page 102:** Spode *Fairy Dell* oval platter from Replacements, Ltd., 800-737-5223, *replacements.com*. **Page 103:** Herend *Chinese Bouquet Rust* dinner plate from Replacements, Ltd., 800-737-5223, *replacements.com*. **Page 105:** Match *1995 Pewter* two-tier

stand, 201-792-5444, *match1995.com*. **Page 106:** Bernardaud *Ecume White* dinner plate, *bernardaud.fr*. **Page 107:** Royal Crown Derby *Derby Posies* teapot from DeVine Corporation, 732-751-0500, *devinecorp.com*. Heritage Lace *Canterbury Classic* table topper, 641-628-4949, *heritagelace.com*. **Page 108:** Lenox *French Perle Ice Blue* 4-piece place setting, 800-223-4311, *lenox.com*. **Page 111:** Shanghai rectangular plate; aqua chambray crochet napkins, 877-967-5362, *worldmarket.com*. **Page 112:** Royal Albert *Lady Carlyle* platter from Replacements, Ltd., 800-737-5223, *replacements.com*. **Page 113:** Pink cake stand from HomeGoods, 800-888-0776, *homegoods.com*.

TEA SANDWICHES AND CANAPÉS

Page 116: Pier1 lace-edge plate and platter, 800-245-4595, *pier1.com*. **Page 117:** White scroll platter from HomeGoods, 800-888-0776, *homegoods.com*. **Pages 118–119:** Minton *Marlow* 3-tiered serving tray, and teapot from Replacements, Ltd., 800-737-5223, *replacements.com*. **Page 120:** Wedgwood *Ascot* salad plate and *Columbia Gold* dinner plate from Replacements, Ltd., 800-737-5223, *replacements.com*. **Page 121:** Annieglass *Ruffle* tray from Bromberg's, 205-871-3276, *brombergs.com*. **Page 122:** Spode *Fairy Dell* oval platter from Replacements, Ltd. 800-737-5223, *replacements.com*. **Page 125:** Vietri *Forma Cloud* rectangular platter, 919-245-4180, *vietri.com*. **Page 126:** Lenox Kate Spade New York *Wickford* oval platter, 800-223-4311, *lenox.com*. **Page 127:** Pier1 gold charger, 800-245-4595, *pier1.com*. Richard Ginori *Siena-Rust* teapot and cup and saucer from Replacements, Ltd., 800-737-5223, *replacements.com*. Candlewick glass platter from Bromberg's, 205-871-3276, *brombergs.com*. **Page 128:** Bella Lux green platter from HomeGoods, 800-888-0776, *homegoods.com*. **Page 129:** Cutwork platter from HomeGoods, 800-888-0776, *homegoods.com*. **Page 131:** Wooden 2-tiered stand, 800-243-0852, *surlatable.com*. **Page 132:** Emile Henry blue rectangular platter, 302-326-4800, *emilehenry.com*. **Page 134:** Annieglass *Ruffle* platter from Bromberg's, 205-871-3276, *brombergs.com*. Raynaud *Allée Royale* teapot from DeVine Corporation, 732-751-0500, *devinecorp.net*. **Page 136:** Villeroy & Boch *Wonderful World Green* service plate from Replacements, Ltd., 800-737-5223, *replacements.com*. Crate & Barrel *Carson* picnic tablecloth, 800-967-6696, *crateandbarrel.com*. **Page 137:** Johnson Brothers *English Chippendale Red/Pink* 5-piece place setting from Replacements, Ltd. 800-737-5223, *replacements.com*. **Page 138:** Vietri *Incanto White Lace* small rectangular platter, 919-245-4180, *vietri.com*. Wedgwood *Sterling* cup and saucer and creamer, 877-720-3486, *wedgwoodusa.com*. **Page 141:** Whitewashed tiered stand, 888-779-5176, *potterybarn.com*. Wedgwood *Nantucket Basket* 5-piece place setting, 877-720-3486, *wedgwoodusa.com*. **Page 142:** Royal Albert *Lady Carlyle* tray from Replacements, Ltd., 800-737-5223, *replacements.com*. **Page 143:** Anna Weatherly sandwich tray from Bromberg's, 205-871-3276, *brombergs.com*. **Page 144:** Ruffled-edge cake stand from HomeGoods, 800-888-0776, *homegoods.com*. **Page 145:** Raynaud *Allée Royale* salad plate and dinner plate from DeVine Corporation, 732-751-0500, *devinecorp.net*. **Page 147:** Wedgwood *Crown Sapphire* salad plate and cup and saucer from Replacements, Ltd., 800-737-5223, *replacements.com*. **Page 148:** Royal Albert *Lady Carlyle* oval platter and cups and saucers from Replacements, Ltd., 800-737-5223, *replacements.com*. Heritage Lace *Canterbury Classic* table topper, 641-628-4949, *heritagelace.com*. **Page 149:** Coalport *Ming Rose* platter from Replacements, Ltd., 800-737-5223, *replacements.com*. Heritage Lace *Canterbury Classic* table topper, 641-628-4949, *heritagelace.com*. **Page 152:** Emile Henry white rectangular platter, 302-326-4800, *emilehenry.com*. **Page 153:** Coalport *Ming Rose* sandwich tray and cup and saucer from Replacements, Ltd., 800-737-5223, *replacements.com*. **Page 154:** Castleton *Sunnyvale* platter from Replacements, Ltd., 800-737-5223, *replacements.com*. Heritage Lace *Canterbury Classic* table topper, 641-628-4949, *heritagelace.com*. **Page 155:** White scroll platter from HomeGoods, 800-888-0776, *homegoods.com*. **Page 158:** Wallace *Baroque Silverplate* cake stand from Replacements, Ltd. 800-737-5223, *replacements.com*.

CAKES AND CUPCAKES

Page 164: Raynaud *Allée Royale* dessert plate, cup and saucer, and teapot from DeVine Corporation, 732-751-0500, *devinecorp.net*. **Page 165:** Minton *Marlow* 3-tiered serving tray, and teapot from Replacements, Ltd., 800-737-5223, *replacements.com*. **Page 166:** Anna Weatherley *Bouquet of Flowers* platter and Garnier-Thiebaut napkin from Bromberg's, 205-871-3276, *brombergs.com*. **Page 169:** Mariposa silver cake stand from Bromberg's, 205-871-3276, *brombergs.com*. Classic lace napkins from Sur La Table, 800-243-0852, *surlatable.com*. **Page 170:** Haviland *Galaxy* bread and butter plate, teapot, and cup and saucer from Replacements, Ltd., 800-737-5223, *replacements.com*. **Page 173:** Royal Doulton Dinnerware 1815 rectangular tray from Macy's, 800-289-6229, *macys.com*. **Page 174:** Juliska *Berry and Thread* cake stand; Anna Weatherley *Anna's Palette* dessert plate from Bromberg's, 205-871-3276, *brombergs.com*. **Page 175:** Herend *Windsor Garden* cup and saucer and bread and butter plate, 800-643-7363, *herendusa.com*. **Page 176:** *Petite Treat* mini pedestals from Rosanna, 877-343-3779, *rosannainc.com*. **Page 177:** Lenox Kate Spade New York *Bissell Cove* accent luncheon plate from Replacements, Ltd., 800-737-5223, *replacements.com*. **Page 178:** Johnson Brothers *Blue Willow* cup and saucer from Replacements, Ltd., 800-737-5223, *replacements.com*. **Page 180:** Lenox *Rose* bread and butter plate and cup and saucer from Replacements, Ltd., 800-737-5223, *replacements.com*. **Page 181:** Bordallo Pinheiro *Rabbit* serving platter and cup and saucer from Replacements, Ltd., 800-737-5223, *replacements.com*.

TARTS AND CHEESECAKES

Page 184: Herend *Chinese Bouquet* cup and saucer; Herend *Chinese Bouquet Garland* dessert plate from Bromberg's, 205-871-3276, *brombergs.com*. **Page 185:** Coastline Imports *Pink Vine* cup and saucer from Stash Tea, 800-800-8327, *stashtea.com*. **Page 186:** Herend *Chinese Bouquet* dessert plate and cup and saucer from Bromberg's, 205-871-3276, *brombergs.com*. **Page 188:** Herend *Princess Victoria* rectangular tray from Bromberg's, 205-871-3276, *brombergs.com*. **Page 190:** Anna Weatherley *Anna's Palette* dessert plate and cup and saucer from Bromberg's, 205-871-3276, *brombergs.com*. **Page 191:** Olympia 3 Tier Glass Cake Plate Stand Server from Amazon, *amazon.com*. Haviland *Louveciennes* cup and saucer from Replacements, Ltd., 800-737-5223, *replacements.com*. **Page 192:** Emile Henry rectangular platter, 302-326-4800, *emilehenryusa.com*. **Page 194:** White scalloped cake plate from Pier1, 800-245-4595, *pier1.com*. Bernardaud *Eden Turquoise* cup and saucer from Replacements, Ltd., 800-737-5223, *replacements.com*. **Page 197:** Annieglass appetizer tray from Bromberg's, 205-871-3276, *brombergs.com*.

COOKIES AND BARS

Pages 200–201: Minton *Marlow* 3-tiered serving tray, and teapot from Replacements, Ltd., 800-737-5223, *replacements.com*. **Page 202:** Appetizer platter from World Market, 877-967-5362, *worldmarket.com*. **Page 204:** Juliska *Berry and Thread* ice-cream compote from Bromberg's, 205-871-3276, *brombergs.com*. **Page 205:** *Tapestry Ocean* dinner napkin from Hen House Linens, 877-717-3595, *henhouselinens.com*. **Page 207:** Wedgwood *Juliet* bread and butter plate, cup and saucer, and teapot from Replacements, Ltd., 800-737-5223, *replacements.com*. **Page 208:** Raynaud *Allée Royale* cup and saucer from DeVine Corporation, 732-751-0500, *devinecorp.net*. **Page 210:** Glass pedestal stands and domes from Pottery Barn, 888-779-5176, *potterybarn.com*. **Page 213:** Emile Henry rectangular platter, 302-326-4800, *emilehenryusa.com*. **Page 214:** Fitz & Floyd *Renaissance Peach* cup and saucer from Replacements, Ltd., 800-737-5223, *replacements.com*. **Page 215:** Wedgwood *Crown Sapphire* footed cup and saucer from Replacements, Ltd., 800-737-5223, *replacements.com*. **Page 217:** Wedgwood *Sterling* salad plate and dinner plate from Replacements, Ltd., 800-737-5223, *replacements.com*. Key lime quilted place mat from Pinecone Hill, 877-586-4771, *pineconehill.com*.

OTHER SWEETS

Page 221: Anna Weatherley *Bouquet of Flowers* tea set from Bromberg's, 205-871-3276, *brombergs.com*. **Page 222:** Herend *Princess Victoria* platter from Bromberg's, 205-871-3276, *brombergs.com*. **Page 223:** Rosenthal Continental *Ancient Beauty* dessert plate from Replacements, Ltd., 800-737-5223, *replacements.com*. **Page 224:** Cake pedestal from Rosanna, 877-343-3779, *rosannainc.com*. **Page 225:** Chas Field Haviland *CHF130* cup and Rosenthal Continental *Ancient Beauty* cup from Replacements, Ltd., 800-737-5223, *replacements.com*. **Page 227:** Royal Doulton Dinnerware *1815* plate from Macy's, 800-289-6229, *macys.com*.

BACK COVER

Tea strainer from Tea for Two, 949-855-1380, *teafortwo.com*. Hutschenreuther *Revere* footed cup and saucer from Replacements, Ltd., 800-737-5223, *replacements.com*.

Editor's Note: *Items not listed are from private collections. No pattern or manufacturer information is available.*

....

CONTRIBUTORS

Photographers: Sarah Arrington, Kimberly Finkel Davis, Kamin H. Williams
Recipe Developers/Food Stylists: Aimee Bishop, Virginia Hornbuckle, Janet Lambert, Chantel Lambeth, Rebecca Treadwell Spradling, Loren Wood
Stylists: Lucy W. Herndon, Lindsey Keith Kessler, Amy Burke Massey, Yukie McLean

....

SPECIALTY TEA PURVEYORS

The teas recommended in the Tea-Pairing Guide on page 11 are available from one or more of these fine companies.

Capital Teas, 888-484-8327, *capitalteas.com*
Elmwood Inn Fine Teas, 800-765-2139, *elmwoodinn.com*
Global Tea Mart, 844-208-2337, *globalteamart.com*
Grace Tea Company, 978-635-9500, *gracetea.com*
Harney & Sons, 888-427-6398, *harney.com*
Mark T. Wendell Tea Company, 978-635-9200, *marktwendell.com*
Simpson & Vail, 800-282-8327, *svtea.com*

Recipe Index

CAKES AND CUPCAKES
Almond-Apple Tea Bread 167
Chocolate-Chai Cake Bites 180
Coconut-Lime Cakes 166
Earl Grey–Chocolate Cakes 177
Flourless Hazelnut Torte with Apricot Preserves 175
Individual Chocolate-Banana Bundt Cakes 170
Italian Cream Cupcakes 176
Orange-Lavender Mini Cupcakes 168
Peanut Butter Pound Cake 168
Petite Strawberry Jam Cakes 164
Red Velvet Mini Cupcakes 171
Spiced Plum Bundt Cake 175
Strawberry-Ginger Roulade 180
Triple-Layer Pumpkin Cakes 179
Vanilla–Sour Cream Fairy Cakes 165
White Chocolate–Lemon Cake 172

CANDIES AND MERINGUES
Brown Sugar–Cashew Fudge 227
Chocolate Truffle Cones with Jasmine Whipped Cream 224
Kiwi, Mango & Coconut Pavlovas 227
Pecan Meringue Drops 220

COOKIES AND BARS
Apricot, Pistachio & Rosemary Biscotti 215
Blueberry Crumb Bars 201
Bonbon Cookies 216
Chocolate-Dipped Peanut Butter Cookies 203
Fig Crumb Bars 203
Ginger-Almond Cookies 204
Greek Easter Cookies (Koulourakia) 204
Key Lime Bars 217
Lemon-Lavender Shortbread 209
Lemon-Lime Spritz Cookies 200
Lemon-Pistachio Shortbread 209
Macadamia–Vanilla Bean Macarons 211
Matcha French Macarons 212
Orange Marmalade Thumbprint Cookies 216
Raspberry French Macarons 211
Stenciled Gingerbread Cookies 215
Strawberry French Madeleines 206
Triple-Layer Brownies 206

ICINGS, FILLINGS, AND SWEET TOPPINGS
Buttercream Frosting 168
Chocolate Glaze 221
Cream Cheese Filling 212
Dark Chocolate Ganache 177
Italian Cream Cheese Frosting 177
Lemon-Mascarpone Filling 172
Lemon–White Chocolate Buttercream 172
Lemon–White Chocolate Mousse 191
Lime Buttercream 166
Meringue Topping 187
Orange–Cream Cheese Frosting 179
Peanut Butter Frosting 169
Semisweet Ganache 197
Strawberry–Cream Cheese Frosting 164
Strawberry-Mascarpone Filling 212
Sweetened Whipped Cream 185
Sweet Rose Icing 40
White Chocolate–Lemon Ganache 211
White Chocolate Hearts 171
Vanilla Buttercream 171
Vanilla Pastry Cream 221
Very Vanilla Buttercream 165

PASTRIES
Caramel Cream Puffs 223
Crostini 135
Éclairs 220
Parmesan Frico Cups 79
Parmesan Wafers 82

PUDDINGS AND SHERBETS
Blackberry-Buttermilk Sherbet 223
Coconut–Vanilla Bean Panna Cottas 225

QUICHES AND SAVORY TARTLETS
Apricot-Chive Chicken Salad in Puff Pastry Shells 103
Apricot, Pecan, and Brie Phyllo Cups 109
Artichoke Frittata 111
Arugula, Lemon, and Gruyère Quiche 96
Asparagus-Prosciutto Crustless Quiche 96
Broccoli Quiche Squares 98
Coq au Vin Tartlets 109
Creamy Crab-Artichoke Tartlets 111
Fresh Herb and Gruyère Quiche 106
Goat Cheese, Date, and Prosciutto Phyllo Cups 112
Ham and Chive Quiches 98
Kale and Sausage Quiches 103
Lobster Salad Barquettes 104
Mushroom and Three-Cheese Tartlets 106
Poppyseed Chicken Tartlets 112
Roasted Red Pepper, Goat Cheese, and Walnut Croustades 94
Smoked Salmon Croustades 101
Spinach-Artichoke Phyllo Cups 104
Tapenade and Cream Cheese Tartlets 94
Tomato-Feta Tartlets 101

SALADS
Baby English Pea Salad in Artichoke Cups 76
Curried Chicken Salad 87
Mini Chicken Taco Salads 81
Petite Potato Salad Flowers 84
Red Quinoa Salad in Frico Cups 75
Salmon-Filled Cucumbers 87
Spring Salad in Frico Cups 79
Watermelon-Feta Salads 82

SAVORY SPREADS, TOPPINGS, AND DRESSINGS
Apple-Beet Slaw 123
Cilantro-Lime Aïoli 152
Citrus Aïoli 139
Corn-Avocado Relish 130
Cracked Pepper and Lemon Double Cream 68
Creamy Honey-Chipotle Dressing 81
Herbed Champagne Vinaigrette 79
Honey-Sherry Vinaigrette 75
Horseradish Aïoli 159
Lemon-Lime Aïoli 120
Lemon-Oregano Aïoli 143
Lemon-Oregano Vinaigrette 146
Smoked Paprika Butter 68
Smoked Paprika-Lime Aïoli 149
Strawberry-Mascarpone Filling 212
Sun-Dried Tomato Aïoli 156
White Balsamic Dressing 130
White Balsamic Vinaigrette 82

SCONES—PLAIN
Sour Cream Scones 19
Vanilla Scones 19

SCONES—ROLLED AND CUT
Apple and Date Scones 43
Blueberry Tea Scones 23
Caraway-Dill Scones 51
Cherry-Rose Scones 30
Chocolate Chip–Cherry Scones 35

Chocolate Chip Scones 35
Cranberry-Pistachio Scones 40
Fig and Honey Scones 33
Gingerbread Scones 43
Gingery Peach Scones 45
Herbed Scones 49
Orange Cream Scones 29
Pear Scones 27
Pimiento Cheese Scones 52
Pistachio Cream Scones 38
Pumpkin Scones 45
Rosemary–White Cheddar Scones 51
Sour Cream Scones 19
Strawberry-Lavender Scones 27
Sweet Potato Scones 36
White Chocolate–Peppermint Scones 33
Zucchini-Parmesan Scones 60

SCONES—SAVORY
Caraway-Dill Scones 51
Herbed Scones 49
Lemon-Basil Scones 49
Pimiento Cheese Scones 52
Rosemary–White Cheddar Scones 51
Savory Tomato-Basil Scones 52
Zucchini-Parmesan Scones 60

SCONES—SWEET
Apple and Date Scones 43
Apricot-Almond Scones 57
Apricot Cream Scones 25
Blueberry-Ginger Scones 57
Blueberry Scones 23
Blueberry Tea Scones 23
Caramel Scones 36
Cherry-Rose Scones 30
Chocolate Chip–Cherry Scones 35
Chocolate Chip Scones 35
Cranberry-Pistachio Scones 40
Dark and White Chocolate Scones 59
Double Chocolate Scones 38
Fig and Honey Scones 33
Gingerbread Scones 43
Gingery Peach Scones 45
Hazelnut Wedge Scones 30
Key Lime Scones 29
Macadamia-Lemon Scones 59
Orange Cream Scones 29
Pear Scones 27
Pecan-Butterscotch Scones 60
Pistachio Cream Scones 38
Pistachio Scones with Sweet Rose Icing 40
Pumpkin Scones 45
Raisin-Orange Scones 25

Strawberry-Lavender Scones 27
Sweet Potato Scones 36
White Chocolate–Peppermint Scones 33

SOUPS
Chilled Cantaloupe Soup 75
Creamy Cauliflower-Leek Soup 82
Creamy Yellow Split Pea and Sweet Potato Soup 91
Curried Tomato Soup 88
Ginger-Carrot Soup 84
Mushroom-Thyme Soup 76
Smoky Chicken and Bean Soup 88
Sweet Pea Soup 91
Tomato Gazpacho 81
Watermelon Gazpacho 79

SWEET SPREADS
Apricot-Honey Butter 68
Brandied Caramel Cream 64
Creamy Lemon Curd 66
Faux Clotted Cream 64
Ginger Curd 66
Maple Butter 69
Molasses-Honey Butter 69
Peppermint Cream 64
Strawberry Curd 66
Strawberry Sweet Cream 64
Sweetened Whipped Cream 68, 185

TARTLETS AND CHEESECAKES
Blueberry-Lemon Mini Cheesecakes 197
Brownie Tart 195
Chocolate Chess Tartlets 185
Chocolate–Peanut Butter Tartlets 193
Decadent Chocolate Mini Cheesecakes 197
Key Lime Mini Cheesecakes 188
Lemon-Chamomile Tartlets 187
Lemon, White Chocolate & Mascarpone Flower Tartlets 190
Peach-Ginger Tartlets 187
Peppermint Mini Cheesecakes 188
Pineapple, Coconut & Macadamia Custard Tartlets 190
Pistachio-Orange Tartlets 195
Strawberry-Mascarpone Tartlets 184
Sweet Potato Tartlets 193

TEA SANDWICHES AND CANAPÉS
Apple, Ham, and Gouda Tea Sandwiches 124
Avocado-Egg Salad Canapés 145
Avocado-Tomatillo Crostini 136
Bacon, Mushroom, and Caramelized Onion Tea Sandwiches 151

Beef and Cheddar Triple-Stack Sandwiches 159
Beef au Poivre and Watercress Tea Sandwiches 126
Broccoli Salad Roulades 130
Buffalo Chicken and Slaw Canapés 139
Caper-Celery Egg Salad Tea Sandwiches 142
Checkerboard Herbed Butter Tea Sandwiches 155
Crab Cake Crostini 120
Creole Egg Salad Tea Sandwiches 117
Cucumber Canapés 124
Cucumber-Pear Canapés 152
Curried Chicken Salad Sandwiches 118
Dilly Roast Beef Tea Sandwiches 149
Flowery Pimiento Cheese Tea Sandwiches 133
Gouda-Goat–Pimiento Cheese Canapés 152
Green Grape and Kiwi Chicken Salad Sandwiches 135
Ham Salad Triple Stacks 117
Herb and Flower Canapés 145
Herbed Egg Salad Flower Sandwiches 118
Italian BLT Tea Sandwiches 142
Mango Chutney–Cucumber Flower Canapés 129
Mini Dill Havarti and Turkey Panini 136
Mini Salmon Croquette Canapés 139
Nutty Carrot, Pineapple, and Ginger Tea Sandwiches 151
Olive-Pecan Finger Sandwiches 120
Pickled Egg Canapés 123
Pickled Okra Roulades 156
Pork Crostini with Corn-Avocado Relish 130
Reuben Canapés 140
Roast Beef Tea Sandwiches with Smoked Paprika–Lime Aïoli 149
Roasted Vegetable–Cream Cheese Tea Sandwiches 140
Shrimp Salad Crostini 135
Smoked Salmon Salad Canapés 155
Smoked Tuna Tea Sandwiches 129
Summertime Ham Sandwiches 156
Tarragon-Shrimp-Salad Finger Sandwiches 133
Tomato, Basil, and Bacon Canapés 126
Vegan Veggie Roulades 146
Walnut-Fig Tea Sandwiches 146

Editor's Note: Recipe titles shown in blue are gluten-free, provided gluten-free versions of processed ingredients (such as flours, extracts, crackers, breads, and broths) are used.